Junctures

in Women's Leadership

⟨ Higher Education ⟩

JUNCTURES

Case Studies in Women's Leadership
Mary K. Trigg, Series Editor

The books in this series explore decisions women leaders make in a variety of fields. Using the case study method, the editors of each volume focus on strategies employed by the women profiled as they face important leadership challenges in business, various social movements, the arts, the health industry, and other sectors. The goal of the series is to broaden our conceptions of what constitutes successful leadership in these changing times.

Junctures
in Women's Leadership

⟨ Higher Education ⟩

Edited by Carmen Twillie Ambar,
Carol T. Christ, and Michele Ozumba

RUTGERS UNIVERSITY PRESS
NEW BRUNSWICK, CAMDEN, AND NEWARK, NEW JERSEY, AND LONDON

Library of Congress Cataloging-in-Publication Data

Names: Ambar, Carmen (Carmen Twillie), editor. | Christ, Carol T., editor. |
Ozumba, Michele, editor.
Title: Junctures in women's leadership : higher education / edited by Carmen
Ambar, Carol Christ, and Michele Ozumba.
Description: New Brunswick : Rutgers University Press, [2020] | Includes bib-
liographical references and index.
Identifiers: LCCN 2019055058 | ISBN 9780813586229 (hardback) |
ISBN 9780813586212 (paperback) | ISBN 9780813586236 (epub) |
ISBN 9780813586243 (pdf) | ISBN 9781978804098 (mobi)
Subjects: LCSH: Women college presidents—United States—Biography. |
Women in higher education—United States—History. | Sex discrimination
in higher education—United States—History. | Educational leadership—
United States.
Classification: LCC LB2341 .J85 2020 | DDC 378.1/01082—dc23
LC record available at https://lccn.loc.gov/2019055058

A British Cataloging-in-Publication record for this book is available from the
British Library.

www.rutgersuniversitypress.org

Manufactured in the United States of America

Contents

Foreword to the Series

Junctures: Case Studies in Women's Leadership

Throughout history, women have always been leaders in their societies and communities. Whether the leadership roles were those of hereditary queens and clan mothers, elected officials, business executives, or founders of organizations, women have participated at the highest levels of decision-making. Yet up through most of the twentieth century, we seldom associated the word *leader* with women. I might even argue that the noun *leader* is one of the most masculinized words in the English language. When we thought of leaders, our minds seldom conjured up women.

Fortunately, there have been recent shifts in our thinking, our images, and our imaginations. In the United States, credit may go to those women in the public eye like Gloria Steinem, Oprah Winfrey, Cecile Richards, and even Eleanor Roosevelt who have blazed new trails in politics, media, and statecraft. Now leadership is beginning to look more gender neutral. That said, it's important to remember that in many parts of the world, women leaders, including prominent feminists, have risen to power more rapidly than seems to be the case here. I think of Gro Brundtland in Norway, Helen Clark in New Zealand, Michelle Bachelet in Chile, and others. These leaders certainly raise new and interesting questions about linking feminism with powerful political leadership. We in the United States also have Sheryl Sandberg to thank for using the word *feminist* in the same sentence as *leadership*.

Despite progress in the past few decades, women have not reached any kind of rough parity with men in terms of positional leadership—that is, the form of leadership that is appointed or elected and recognized as powerful and influential in coeducational public life. Women continue to be dramatically underrepresented in all major domains of leadership from politics to Fortune 500 companies, labor unions, and academic administration, and even in fields where they are the majority like health care, teaching, or the arts. Scholars like Deborah Rhode and Nannerl O. Keohane note that at the rate the United States is going, there will not be a "convergence toward parity" for an additional three centuries. Given the need for outstanding leadership at all levels and sectors of society and the huge waste of talent that exists when so many capable women are not encouraged to move into senior leadership positions, we cannot afford to wait for parity even three decades, let alone three centuries!

If we wish to accelerate the process of gender parity in leadership in the twenty-first century, what steps might we take and what role can academia play in helping increase the pool and percentage of women leaders? Historically, women's colleges, according to pioneering research by Elizabeth Tidball and others, graduated disproportionate numbers of women leaders up through the 1970s. More recently, business schools, which were largely male bastions, have educated a share of women leaders.

Today, in interdisciplinary fields such as women's and gender studies, examining the concept of "leadership" and teaching women students to be more effective leaders in a given profession or context is highly contested. For example, *Ms*. noted that in 2011, "only a handful of the more than 650 women's studies programs at colleges and universities provide[d] practical and theoretical knowledge necessary for the next generation to make a significant impact on their communities and world" as leaders. Many feminists and women scholars have negative associations with traditional ideas of leadership, arguing that the concept is elitist, individualistic, and hierarchical, as well as that it justifies putting work ahead of family and parenting. Moreover, traditional leadership studies often have failed to take account of structural and contextual frameworks of unequal power and privilege, especially around gender and race. And yet approaching the study of leadership with a gender-sensitive lens is crucial if we are to make more progress toward a fairer and more just distribution of power and opportunity for women and men alike.

This brings us to the genesis of this series, Junctures in Women's Leadership. The volumes in the series are designed to provide insights into the decision-making process undertaken by women leaders, both well known and deserving to be better known. The case studies run the gamut from current affairs to the past. The Rutgers Institute for Women's Leadership (IWL) consortium, a group of nine separate units at the university including Douglass Residential College, the Department of Women's and Gender Studies, and the Center for American Women in Politics, is sponsoring this series as a way to provide new pedagogical tools for understanding leadership exercised by women. Each volume will consist of a dozen or so case studies of leaders in a specific field of endeavor. The focus is not on the woman leader per se but rather on the context that surrounded her decision, the factors she considered in making the decision, and the aftermath of the decision. Also, even though the series is focused on decision-making by women leaders, it is not designed to demonstrate that all decisions were good ones or yielded the results expected.

The series does not promote the notion that there are biologically determined differences between women's and men's decision-making practices. There is no such thing as a "women's" approach to leadership. Nothing universally characterizes women's approaches to leadership as opposed to men's. Neither gender is genetically wired to be one kind of leader as opposed to another. That kind of biologically determined, reductionist thinking has no place in this series. Nor does the series suggest that women make decisions according to a single set of "women's values or issues," though there is some evidence to suggest that once women reach a critical mass of decision-makers, they tend to elevate issues of family and human welfare more than men. This evidence, collected by Rutgers

University's Center for American Women in Politics, also suggests that women are more likely to seek compromise across rigid ideologies than men in the same position.

Our series of case studies on women in leadership is not designed to prove that simply electing or appointing women to leadership positions will miraculously improve the standard of living for all people. Few of us believe that. On the other hand, it is important to examine some questions that are fundamental to understanding the values and practices of women leaders who, against the odds, have risen to shape the worlds in which we all live. The series employs the "case study" method because it provides concrete, real-life examples of women leaders in action. We hope the case studies will prompt many questions, not the least of which is, What fresh perspectives and expanded insights do women bring to leadership decisions? And more theoretical and controversial, Is there a feminist model of leadership?

In conclusion, the IWL is delighted to bring these studies to the attention of faculty, students, and leaders across a wide range of disciplines and professional fields. We believe it will contribute to accelerating the progress of women toward a more genuinely gender-equal power structure in which both men and women share the responsibility for forging a better and more just world for generations to come.

Alison R. Bernstein
Director, Institute for Women's Leadership Consortium
Professor of history and women's and gender studies
Rutgers University / New Brunswick
April 2015

New Foreword to the Series
Junctures: Case Studies in
Women's Leadership

The last time I saw Alison Bernstein was at a book launch party
for the first two volumes in the Junctures series in the late spring
of 2016. Sadly, on June 30 of that year, Alison—director of the
Institute for Women's Leadership (IWL), professor of history and
women's and gender studies at Rutgers, and original editor of the
Junctures series, which is sponsored by the IWL—died. The first
volume, *Junctures in Women's Leadership: Social Movements*, which
she and I coedited, was published one month before Alison's death.
(The second volume, which focuses on women's leadership in business, was published simultaneously.) The day before she died, I
was visiting the progressive, independent City Lights Bookstore
in San Francisco and saw our newly published Junctures volume
on the shelf. I texted Alison a photograph of the book because
I knew it would please her. Her former colleagues at the Ford
Foundation—where she served first as a program officer, later as
director of the Education and Culture program, and then as vice
president for Knowledge, Creativity, and Freedom and its successor
program Education, Creativity, and Free Expression—described Alison as "a powerful voice for justice" and "a ferocious defender of and
advocate for the rights of women and girls."[1] In its illumination of
women leading change across a range of contexts, including social
movements, business, the arts, higher education, public health,
science, politics, and media, the Junctures in Women's Leadership
series carries these feminist and egalitarian impulses forward. It

also does this with its advocacy of gender parity and its message that for women to take their full place as leaders, our expectations and stereotypes about leadership must change.

The Junctures series seeks to redress the underrepresentation of women in leadership positions and to suggest a different kind of future. Although quick to denounce a "women's" approach to leadership, Alison did note that research indicates that once women reach a critical mass of decision-makers, they tend to elevate issues of family and human welfare more than men do. In addition, the Junctures series suggests that when women wield power and hold decision-making positions, they transform organizations, ideas, industries, institutions, culture, and leadership itself.[2] Women's lived experiences are distinct from men's, and their lives collide with history in unique ways. Moreover, the diversity of experience among women further enriches their perspectives. This influences how they lead: for example, women broaden art and museum collections to include more work by women and by artists from diverse backgrounds. This is not insignificant. The arts volume makes a persuasive case for the necessity of women artists and arts professionals in leadership positions to advance gender parity in the arts. "Women leaders make a difference," its editors conclude.[3] Similarly, the editors of the business volume determine that "from their [women leading change in business] experiences come unique business ideas and the passion to address women's needs and interests."[4] Each volume, in its way, illustrates this.

The Junctures series aims to capture women's leadership in action and at pivotal junctures or moments of decision-making. Its goal is to broaden our conceptions of what constitutes successful leadership in these changing times. Our approach is intersectional: we consider gender, race, class, ethnicity, and physical and social location, as well as how they influence access to and the practice of leadership. We wander through time and historical context and consider multiple ways of leading. Authors and editors of each volume conducted multiple interviews with the living subjects, which make this compendium a contribution to academic scholarship on women's leadership. Collectively the volumes contemplate the ways that gender conventions influenced how some women have practiced leadership, the pain and impetus of gender and/or racial discrimination and exclusion, and the challenges some women leaders have faced as mothers and primary caretakers of home and children.

We use the format of the "case study" broadly. Each essay or case study is organized into a "Background" section, which describes the protagonist's rise to leadership and lays out a decision-making juncture or problem, and a "Resolution" section, which traces the ways the leader "resolved" the problem or juncture, as well as her legacy. Each volume considers what prepared these particular women for leadership, highlights personal strategies and qualities, and investigates the ways that family, education, mentors, personal injustice, interaction with social movements, and pivotal moments in history shaped these protagonists' approaches and contributions as leaders in varied contexts. We have sought to cast a wide net and gather examples from the United States as well as around the world (the first three volumes include case studies from Kenya, Nicaragua, South Africa, the United Kingdom, and Laos). Necessarily, volume editors have had to make difficult decisions about who to include and exclude. Our goal is to offer a rich abundance of diverse examples of women's leadership and the difference it makes rather than a comprehensive theory about women's leadership or even what feminist leadership might entail. We seek to prompt questions as well as provide answers.

Alison and I stated in the preface to the social movements volume that some of the qualities that fuel leadership include "courage, creativity, passion and perseverance."[5] Alison Bernstein exemplified all of these qualities. "She was wild, clear, and shameless," Ken Wilson, Alison's former colleague at the Ford Foundation, wrote of her.[6] The same could be said of many of the audacious and brave change makers in this series. The IWL sends their stories out into the world to document and preserve them and to educate and inspire faculty, students, and leaders across a range of fields and disciplines. We hope these volumes will inform those who aspire to leadership and apprize those who practice it. Leadership has the potential to forge gender and racial equity, to bring about innovative solutions, and to advance social justice.

Mary K. Trigg
Faculty Director of Leadership Programs and Research, Institute
for Women's Leadership Consortium
Associate Professor and Chair, Department of
Women's and Gender Studies
Rutgers University / New Brunswick
October 2017

Notes

1. Margaret Hempel, "Remembering Alison Bernstein," Ford Foundation, July 11, 2016, https://www.fordfoundation.org/ideas/equals-change-blog/posts/remembering-alison-bernstein/.
2. Lisa Hetfield and Dana M. Britton, *Junctures in Women's Leadership: Business* (New Brunswick, N.J.: Rutgers University Press, 2016), xi.
3. Judith Brodsky and Ferris Olin, *Junctures in Women's Leadership: The Arts* (New Brunswick, N.J.: Rutgers University Press, 2018), xv.
4. Hetfield and Britton, *Junctures: Business*, xiii.
5. Mary K. Trigg and Alison R. Bernstein, *Junctures in Women's Leadership: Social Movements* (New Brunswick, N.J.: Rutgers University Press, 2016), xii. This insight is drawn from Linda Gordon, "Social Movements, Leadership, and Democracy: Toward More Utopian Mistakes," *Journal of Women's History* 14, no. 2 (2002): 104.
6. Hempel, "Remembering Alison Bernstein."

Preface

With the rapid pace of change in higher education today, it is helpful to study accounts of senior leaders who have had to confront challenges, make bold decisions, and employ strategies to address complex issues. This is particularly true regarding women leaders, who bring a gender lens to their stories. In 1986, women comprised 9 percent of all college presidents. In 2013, women comprised 33 percent of the leaders at community colleges, 23 percent at four-year colleges, and 22 percent at doctoral universities.[1] These figures remained fairly constant through 2017 when women made up 30 percent of American college presidents, although women of color comprised only a scant 5 percent.[2]

This volume in the Junctures: Case Studies in Women's Leadership series features women leaders in higher education whose stories reveal ways in which they navigated both internal and external challenges to their institutions and how they used their influence and power to bring about institutional transformation. In twelve chapters, this book presents the powerful stories of a diverse group of women who have served as presidents of many kinds of institutions—private liberal arts colleges, public and private universities, women's colleges, and large urban community colleges. One exception is Bernice Sandler. Sandler led the historic research and advocacy campaign that resulted in the enactment of Title IX federal legislation, the first legislation to ever address sex discrimination in education. According to Sandler, "The [phrase] 'sex discrimination' was relatively new in the 1960s and 1970s. . . .

You didn't think about a pattern. It's just individual instances here and there."[3]

The racial and gender disparities that continue to exist in higher education leadership make the stories in this volume even more compelling. This is especially so when one considers the essential role of presidents in shaping an institution's culture, strategic direction, and spirit of innovation and adaptation to today's increasingly diverse student population and globalized society.

All the women profiled in this book brought with them to the presidency their lived experiences as well as their academic and professional achievements. They were selected because their careers illustrate various pathways to leadership. The reader will gain insights into the roles of family, mentors, colleagues, and the external sociopolitical environment that influenced their journeys to executive leadership. A few examples describe some of these lived experiences.

As an anthropologist, Johnnetta Cole brought insights into southern culture to create a new climate of shared governance at Spelman College and leveraged the college's history of social activism to define Spelman as the top choice for brilliant African American women. The result was tripling the endowment and putting Spelman on the map as one of the top private liberal arts colleges in the country: "I had to reconnect with my southernness. I had not lived in the South since that one year at Fisk, 1953 to '54. And so, I really took some counsel there with myself, and I started reading about and thinking about 'What is the nature of being Southern?' And once I reconnected with a good deal of that, I'm not saying that it solved the problem, but it helped me to administer far better. Secondly, I really think that my own openness was useful. It made me accessible. It diffused some of the sense of 'Here comes the president.'"

Jill Kerr Conway's vision for Smith College included a deep desire to provide opportunities for adult women to complete their college degrees. In her words, "What could be achieved if an elite college for women began to take older women seriously, to give them financial aid and all the services necessary to maximize their talents? . . . Underneath all these questions was my sadness that my super intelligent mother had never had the chance for an education she'd have used so well. . . . She was the reason I'd never stopped trying to expand women's opportunities." This passionate commitment to educating adult women led to the establishment of the Ada Comstock Scholars Program that continues to flourish at Smith College today.[4]

As the first African American president of an Ivy League institution, Ruth Simmons arrived at Brown University with an impressive career in academic leadership, including serving as president of Smith College. Her signature achievement at Brown was establishing the Slavery and Justice Committee to research the university's historic relationship to the transatlantic slave trade. This initiative is an example of the intersection of personal and academic experience informing Simmons's decision-making process. Reflecting on her work, she said, "It felt like the right decision. It didn't feel like a bold decision. . . . In universities, we're just constantly wrestling with trying to make the right decision day after day. . . . Sometimes they have weight and sometimes they don't, but it's very much the way I try to live my life."

Many of the women featured in this book came of age in the era of the civil rights and women's rights movements and saw their leadership roles as effecting social change. Nancy Cantor's commitment to diversity and inclusion shaped her work defending affirmative action as provost at the University of Michigan. She also led the call to remove Chief Illiniwek as the mascot when she was chancellor of Illinois University-Urbana Champaign. She said, "For me, it would be impossible to do these jobs if I didn't feel that my public voice and change-making proclivity couldn't at least be partly there."

Through these women's leadership journeys, readers will gain insights into the unique challenges each leader faced as well as some of the common themes that shaped their experiences as distinct from men: differences in expectations, criticism, support, and identity. At the same time, these women demonstrate their ability to manage the full scope of responsibility in senior positions by surmounting significant barriers, building strategic alliances, and making measurable impacts that define their tenures as presidents.

The chapters are organized into three groups. The first five chapters emphasize a cultural lens, describing actions and decisions that influenced cultural norms in regard to gender, ethnic diversity, access, and community/university relationships. Included in this section are Bernice Sandler, Ruth Simmons, Nancy Cantor, Nannerl Keohane, and Molly Broad. The next three chapters, including Jill Conway, Johnnetta Cole, and Hannah Gray, emphasize a social lens; these leaders devoted themselves to activities that elevated their institutions' identities and repositioned their institutions' academic standings. The last four chapters emphasize a structural lens, describing decisions and actions that led to a significant transformation in institutional and administrative systems. The subjects of these final chapters are Judith Shapiro, Regina Peruggi, Patricia McGuire, and Juliet García.

Each woman's story is her own; nevertheless, there are themes that emerge from their experiences as leaders and college presidents. While there are unique circumstances associated with each president's situation, collectively, these women leaders demonstrate a strong commitment to collaboration, participatory leadership, integrity, academic excellence, and social responsibility. We hope readers gain insight into the complexities of contemporary women's academic leadership as well as the internal and external dimensions of effective decision-making. Finally, we hope readers come away inspired by these stories of courage and determination to make a positive difference for all in higher education.

Carmen Twillie Ambar, Carol T. Christ, and Michele Ozumba

Notes

1 Tiffani Lennon, *Benchmarking Women's Leadership in the United States* (Denver: Colorado Women's College, University of Denver, 2013).

2 See the 2017 American College President Study by the American Council on Education, accessed April 13, 2020, https://www.acenet.edu/Research-Insights/Pages/American-College-President-Study.aspx.

3 D. Rose, "Regulating Opportunity: Title IX and the Birth of Gender-Conscious Higher Education Policy," *Journal of Policy History* 27, no. 1 (2015): 157–183.

4 Auden Thomas, "Welfare Women Go Elite: The Ada Comstock Scholars Program," *NASPA Journal about Women in Higher Education* 1, no. 1 (2009): 105–124.

Junctures

in Women's Leadership

⟨ Higher Education ⟩

Too Strong for a Woman
Bernice Sandler and the Birth of Title IX

Leslee A. Fisher

> It will take many generations because what we
> are now talking about is not just increased oppor-
> tunities for girls and women but about a social
> revolution with an impact as large as the Industrial
> Revolution, for we are changing the roles of women
> and men, so that they are far closer to equal than
> they have ever been in the history of the world, and
> that is not easy to do. We have only taken the very
> *first steps* of what will be a very long journey.

> —Bernice Resnick Sandler, speech given at Women
> Rock: Title IX Academic and Legal Conference at
> Cleveland State University, March 30, 2007

Background

Bernice Resnick Sandler was born in New York City on March 3,
1928, and grew up in Brooklyn in a family of German and Russian
immigrants.[1] To her friends, she's known as Bunny—a nickname
based on the Yiddish version of Bernice, or Bunya by translation.[2]
In 1948, Sandler graduated cum laude with a BS in psychology from
Brooklyn College.[3] In 1950, she obtained a master's degree in clinical
and school psychology from the City College of New York. And in
1960, she completed her EdD in counseling and personnel services
from the University of Maryland.

Before Sandler decided to become an activist in the fight against gender discrimination in higher education, she describes how she, like many women during the mid to late 1960s, was reluctant to believe that there was such a thing as gender discrimination in the workplace. She also didn't join the women's movement because she thought that feminists were "unfeminine," "radical," "man-hating," and "abrasive," buying into stereotypes produced by the media to dissuade women from engaging in the feminist movement.[4]

Sandler's illusion of a perfect (i.e., gender-equal) world was shattered in 1969, when she graduated with her doctorate from the University of Maryland. Although already working as a part-time lecturer in the department, she was not seriously considered for any of the seven full-time openings available at the time of her graduation. When she asked a male faculty member why she wasn't considered for these positions, he stated, "Let's face it, you come on too strong for a woman."[5] Sandler went home and cried; further, she recalls, "[I] blamed myself for speaking up a few times at staff meetings. I blamed myself for discussing professional issues with faculty members. I regretted my participation in classes as a graduate student. In short, I accepted the assessment that I was, indeed, too strong for a woman."[6]

In the months following this incident, she twice was denied an academic job. As Sandler puts it, it felt like there was never a good time to hire a woman in academia: "Number one, I was older; number two, I had children, and my children were in school . . . it was . . . a catch-22 because when you're younger, they don't want to hire you because you'll get married. When you do get married, then they don't want to hire you because now you're going to have children. . . . I mean it, there are rationalizations for women all along the job path so that . . . there was really [never] a good time to hire women."[7]

It was through the betrayal of not being hired in an academic position that Sandler began to awaken to the issue of gender discrimination in the workplace. Even though she felt betrayed at first, she decided to do something about the betrayal. As Sandler states, "When things go wrong in my life, I start to read about the problem. I am a great believer in bibliotherapy, so I began to read about the law and sex discrimination, although I had never had the slightest interest in law other than considering a career as a legal secretary for a short time when I was in high school. I naively assumed that because sex discrimination was wrong, it must be, therefore, illegal. It was not."[8]

Sandler's bibliotherapy included reading the Equal Pay Act of 1963, Title VII of the Civil Rights Act of 1964, and the Fourteenth Amendment.[9] What she discovered was that in all three of these documents, women are excluded. For example, although the Equal Pay Act of 1963 included men who were in professional and executive jobs such as administrators, faculty, and teachers at all educational levels, females were not covered. In addition, although Title VII of the Civil Rights Act of 1964 prohibited employment discrimination on the basis of sex, race, color, religion, and national origin, it specifically excluded educational institution employees "in their educational activities."[10] This meant that women and girls (including females of color) were not protected in federally assisted programs on the basis of their sex. And while the Fourteenth Amendment claimed to offer all persons equal protection under the law,[11] it had not been regarded as, in any way, relevant to sex discrimination.

Sandler's eureka moment came as she was reading a report prepared by the U.S. Commission on Civil Rights evaluating the enforcement of civil rights legislation. As she describes it, "I started reading about African Americans and how they had gained, were beginning to gain, a lot of freedoms [through] a lot of lawsuits, and things were beginning to change. And so they were like a good role model [to fight sex discrimination]."

She continues, "And I found a loophole in terms of contract compliance, and that made all the difference." Further, she states, "There was a footnote, and being an academic, I read footnotes, so I turned to the back of the book to read it. The footnote stated that Executive Order 11246 had recently been amended to cover sex discrimination by Executive Order 11375. I was alone at home, and it was a genuine eureka moment. I actually shrieked aloud, for I immediately realized that many universities and colleges had federal contracts [and] were therefore subject to the sex-discrimination provisions of the executive order and that the order could be used to fight sex discrimination on American campuses."

Sandler persevered. She chose to head directly into the eye of the storm.[12] She filed administrative charges of sex discrimination against 250 colleges and universities under Executive Order 11246.[13] As she recalls, some of the storms she faced while doing her Title IX work included that "it was hard to convince a lot of people that even though [discrimination against African Americans] wasn't the same [as sex discrimination], it was still . . . discrimination. . . . Also, a lot of people, in terms of how they viewed men and women, saw these things as inborn."

She also clarifies, "You did not have to be an attorney to file a complaint. You could literally say, 'I am charging X university with sex discrimination, and here is some evidence.' . . . You didn't need a lot. . . . I would use a minimal thing, you know, [things like] 25 percent of graduates in psychology are women, but they only hold 5 percent of the jobs in psychology. [I'm making up these figures now] . . . but I would be gathering data to document that there really was sex discrimination and that we needed to do something about it."

All Sandler's work was volunteer; she did not get paid for using her research skills and training to gather data, find loopholes, or file sex-discrimination complaints.

Sandler was also bolstered by the fact that she was married and supported financially by her husband. As she puts it, "I was safely married at the time. . . . The marriage was not dependent upon my income. . . . If I lost my job, it didn't matter." Sandler further specifies, "It didn't cost any money to make [these charges]; you just write it up. But I was not going to lose anything because I was married, and at that point, being married meant you didn't have to work in many instances if you were middle class. . . . If you were a single person, you couldn't afford to take that risk. . . . I was able to afford to take that risk."

To be sure, the 250 institutions that Sandler filed sex-discrimination complaints against were not thrilled with her work. As Sandler indicates, "Oh, well, people in higher education were certainly not happy." In addition, most of the formal complaints that she filed against these institutions were "subsequently lost by the government."[14] Furthermore, as Sandler reflects, "Like many laws, it is up to the courts to determine what the law actually means concerning a variety of issues."[15]

Sandler also recognizes the value in letting other people lend her a hand. For example, she was a member of the Women's Equity Action League (WEAL), founded by Ohio attorney Elizabeth Boyer, and became chair of its Federal Action Contract Compliance Committee; in fact, she was the only member of the committee.[16] It was through WEAL that Sandler filed the first administrative class-action complaint against *all* colleges and universities receiving federal contracts in January of 1970.

WEAL and Sandler were also aided in the endeavor to end sex discrimination by Vincent Macaluso, director of the Office for Federal Contract Compliance at the Department of Labor. As Sandler put it, his help was "secret and very substantial."[17] It was fortuitous for Sandler to end up partnering with Macaluso. As she states, "Fortunately, I hooked up with [Macaluso]. . . . [He] worked at the Labor Department [and] had actually written the federal regulations concerning sex discrimination and contractors. . . . He was delighted to see me because he had been wanting someone to do something about it. So he actually ended up practically writing most of the first complaints that I filed because I certainly had no legal background whatsoever . . . but he taught me what I needed to do and how to do it."

At this time, some women's organizations began filing sex-discrimination charges, and other women began contacting Sandler about their own institutions.[18] Sandler would tell them to compile data related to the number and percentage, at each rank, of women faculty in several departments, including their own. She would then compare their university-specific compiled data against the total number of doctorates awarded to U.S. women in these specific fields; she used this comparison as the foundation for her filed administrative complaints with the U.S. Department of Labor.[19]

In a stroke of brilliance, Macaluso also encouraged Sandler to tell the women who were contacting her to write letters to their two state senators and their congressional representatives, asking them to write the secretaries of the then Department of Health, Education, and Welfare and the Department of Labor, respectively.[20] The goal was to have the secretaries enforce Executive Order 11246 as well as to keep senators and representatives abreast regarding whether sexual discrimination complaints had been resolved. It was brilliant because congressional staffs then became aware that there was sexual discrimination in education. The letters also alerted federal agency staff to the issue.[21] In fact, as Sandler writes, "We generated so much Congressional mail that the Departments of Labor and Health, Education and Welfare had to assign several full-time personnel to handle the letters."[22]

In April 1970, four months after Sandler enlisted the aid of women in a letter-writing campaign about enforcing Executive Order 11246, both the University of Michigan and Harvard University were the first to be federally investigated for sex discrimination. This meant that because of Sandler's and others' efforts, there was now direct involvement from the U.S. government in investigating college and university sex discrimination.[23] As Sandler writes, "Pandora's box had finally been opened."[24]

Throughout this process, Sandler met another key helper: Representative and Democrat Edith Green from Oregon. Sandler says, "I'm the godmother, but she's the real mother of Title IX." Sandler describes how Green had first worked as a teacher and was then elected to Congress: "She had been there long enough, and in those days, everything in the Congress was managed by seniority. . . . She was in a safe district and got reelected and reelected, which gave her more tenure in terms of moving up the ladder in those days. You got to be head of a committee simply by being there long enough . . . [and] she knew about discrimination in education."

Because Green had witnessed educational discrimination firsthand, she wanted to amend the assorted antidiscrimination laws so that they would cover girls and women in educational settings.[25] Since Green was the chair of the Committee on Education and Labor's Special Subcommittee on Education, she had the authority to initiate the legislation that eventually became Title IX.[26] What she lacked were the constituency and data. What Sandler provided Green was "the constituency (the newly developing advocacy groups and active individuals) and the data she needed (often data collected by women about their campuses or professions)."[27]

As Sandler specifies, "I began sending [Green] copies, met with her staff. . . . Many people were not aware of how widespread the discrimination was, and . . . we . . . began to document it. . . . She was very interested because I was documenting sex discrimination, which nobody had really done before. And it wasn't that hard because it's just simple statistics. But now there was interest in the subject and a way to file charges because most institutions receive federal funds of one sort or another . . . and so it opens up the door. . . . Now there are things you can do about it."

In addition, Sandler helped create new language to talk about the issue: *sex discrimination*. As she states, "A lot of people were a bit aware of it, but now we have the words *sex discrimination*." She also describes how men became important allies in the fight to end sex discrimination in educational institutions. As she details, "There were lots of men who were very helpful because they had wives who were professionals. And so they understood exactly what [was going on]. . . . They knew their wives' stories, how important it was to get people aware of this."

When Representative Green introduced the bill that would become Title IX, she decided to hold congressional hearings. These were the first-ever hearings related to discrimination against women in the educational workplace.[28] At those congressional hearings, Sandler gave overview testimony to the committee from 1,200 pages of data she had collected related to sex discrimination in education.

Sandler was also the one who suggested most of the witnesses to Green.[29] Witness voices and stories are powerful because they embody experiences that are hard to imagine until they are spoken out loud. As Sandler writes, "The witnesses provided horror stories, mainly about women employed on campus such as departments refusing to hire women or refusing to promote them or give them tenure; or women who received many thousands of dollars less salary than their male counterparts; or women working full-time as faculty, with no benefits, no office, no salary, because their husbands also taught at the same university."[30] In addition, numerous women of color described the impact of sex discrimination on minority women. Sandler concluded, "It was an eye opener for anyone who saw it."[31]

After the hearings were over, Sandler was hired by Representative Green to put together a written record of the hearings. Because of this request, Sandler became the first person appointed to a congressional committee staff to work specifically on women's issues.[32] Nothing like this had ever happened; never before had so much information on sex discrimination been assembled, let alone published.[33]

One final note: because there was limited awareness about the extent of educational sex discrimination, there was also limited understanding about what Title IX could do about it. As Sandler puts it, "Even those of us intimately involved in Title IX . . . did not fully understand its impact at the time."[34]

In fact, as related to collegiate extracurricular activities like sports, there was very little interest by those in Washington about what Title IX might do. As Sandler recalls, "When Title IX was close to passage, there were about five or six of us (plus Rep. Green) who realized that Title IX would cover sports and athletics."[35] Even Sandler's own understanding of Title IX's potential impact on sports was narrow; as she reflected, she thought at the time, "Isn't this nice! Because of Title IX, at the annual field-day events in schools, there will be more activities for girls."[36]

In addition, when Senator Birch Bayh (also a member of WEAL's advisory board and a Democrat from Indiana) introduced the bill in the Senate, although one senator required reassurance that girls and women would not be allowed to play football, other senators were more focused on the impact that Title IX might have on college beauty pageants, sororities, and fraternities.[37] Interestingly, even though most people now associate Title IX with collegiate athletics, aside from physical educators at the kindergarten through grade twelve and collegiate levels as well as coaches, very few people had an understanding of the ways that Title IX would impact girls' and women's sport participation.

Resolution

Title IX of the Educational Amendments of 1972 was signed into law by President Richard M. Nixon on June 23, 1972, after it was passed by the Ninety-Second Congress.[38] It reads, "No person in the United States shall, on the basis of sex, be excluded from participation in, be denied the benefits of, or be subjected to discrimination under any education program or activity receiving federal financial assistance."[39]

The scope of Title IX extends to *all* U.S. state and local educational agencies and institutions that receive Department of Education federal financial assistance.[40] This includes approximately 7,000 postsecondary institutions and 16,500 local school districts—as well as for-profit schools, museums, libraries, and education and vocational rehabilitation agencies—in all fifty states, possessions, and territories of the U.S. and the District of Columbia. In addition, educational activities and programs and activities receiving the Department of Education federal funds must "operate in a nondiscriminatory manner."[41]

The passage of Title IX accomplished a great many things. For example, Sandler's compilation of material and the efforts of Vincent Macaluso (director of the Department of Labor's Office for Federal Contract Compliance), Edith Green (chair of the House of Representatives' Committee on Education and Labor), and Senator Birch Bayh (Democrat, Indiana, who introduced the bill in the Senate) resulted in the following:[42]

- Both women and men became more aware of educational sex discrimination.
- Because of this awareness, women became a new and vitally important advocacy group.
- Most of the unconcealed practices, policies, and programs that treated girls and women differently or excluded them were abolished.
- The ambition, self-esteem, and confidence of millions of girls and women increased after Title IX was passed.
- Issues of import to girls and women became institutionalized.

- Data and research related to discrimination against girls and women became viewed as legitimate knowledge.
- The interests and needs of diverse groups of women were considered important and legitimate areas of concern.
- Girls' and women's sport interest and participation skyrocketed.[43] In fact, recent statistics demonstrate that in the first thirty years following Title IX's passage (1972–2002), there was an increase in female high school varsity sport participation from 7 percent to 41.5 percent, and 2.8 million girls participated in high school athletics overall. In addition, by 2001, 150,900 female athletes participated in collegiate athletics, making up 43 percent of collegiate athletes in general.[44]

Sandler believes there are still many issues that need to be tackled related to sex discrimination. For example, she notes, "In many places, men's sports get more [funding]. . . . Even if you take away football, there's not equality . . . and it varies from school to school or school system to school system." When reflecting on when Title IX was passed, Sandler says,

I was quite naïve. I thought all the problems of sex discrimination in education would be solved in one or two years at most. When two years passed, I increased my estimate to five years, then later to ten, then to fifty, and now I realize it will take many generations to solve all the problems. We began with simple goals. . . . We had only limited information about the extent of sex discrimination at that time, and we did not fully understand how comprehensive . . . complex . . . [and] subtle . . . sex discrimination is.[45]

Further, Sandler believes that there is still sex discrimination that needs to be addressed:[46]

- Sex discrimination is not paid as much attention to at the high school, middle school, and elementary school levels as it is at the college level.

- Title IX enforcement by the Office for Civil Rights at the Education Department is severely backlogged, typically delayed, and spotty at best.
- Participation in sports is still a major issue. Discrepancies in equipment, facilities, opportunities, scholarships, and so on still exist.
- Attorneys and judges need more training about Title IX, since many have negligible knowledge of this area of the law, including its implications.
- More sexual harassment programs and training are needed in school systems, particularly related to student-on-student sexual harassment.
- Changes to Title IX (including allowing single-sex programs and classes) need monitoring.[47]

Despite pushback, Sandler does not believe that Title IX will be dismantled. As she states, "Oh, there are always people who would like to dismantle it. But it's too far. It's too ingrained now . . . There was a time when that was a real possibility. But I think it would be very hard to dismantle, partly because for every woman who's in sports . . . you have fathers whose daughters are playing sports . . . and [fathers] made a difference in the civil rights movement . . . There's now a whole history of participation by women and girls, and people expect them to be treated differently [now]." Most importantly, Sandler emphasized, "It would be illegal."

In closing, as the heroine of her own story, Sandler faced the world of education head-on, saw the inequities contained within it, challenged them, and came out the other side with "a new understanding of . . . [that] world" and herself.[48] She realized that the personal was indeed political, that by challenging the male/female binary in higher education, she and other women (as well as male allies) could work together to make the educational workplace a more just and equitable place for women.

When asked what she would tell a young feminist advocate, Sandler states, "There . . . [are] still discrepancies that happen, but people have a way of protesting, and then they can be changed. . . .

It's not like it used to be. . . . Women themselves are activists now. . . . They know enough about the law and Title IX, and they recognize . . . inequality in a different way. . . . They see it, and they can do something about it."

Notes

1 See "All about Bernice Sandler" on her official website, http://www .bernicesandler.com/id2.htm.
2 "Bernice R. Sandler, Ed.D. (1928–2019)," Archives of Maryland, accessed April 26, 2018, http://msa.maryland.gov/megafile/msa/speccol/sc3500/ sc3520/015200/015244/html/15244bio.html.
3 Jeahlisa Bridgeman, "Profile: Bernice Resnick Sandler," Psychology's Feminist Voices, 2014, last updated 2019, https://feministvoices.com/bernice-resnick -sandler/.
4 Bernice Resnick Sandler, "Title IX: How We Got It and What a Difference It Made," Cleveland State Law Review 55, no. 40 (2007): 473–489, https:// engagedscholarship.csuohio.edu/clevstlrev/vol55/iss4/4/.
5 Ibid.
6 Ibid.
7 Bernice Sandler, in discussion with the author, May 2, 2018. All direct quotes are taken from this interview unless otherwise noted.
8 Sandler, "Title IX."
9 Ibid.
10 Ibid.
11 Ibid.
12 Victoria Schmidt, "The Heroine's Journey Arc," Heroine Journey Project (blog), accessed March 2015 https://heroinejourneys.com/heroine-journey-ii/.
13 Sandler, "Title IX."
14 Ibid.
15 Ibid.
16 Ibid.
17 Ibid.
18 Ibid.
19 Ibid.
20 Ibid.
21 Ibid.
22 Ibid.
23 Ibid.
24 Ibid.
25 Ibid.
26 Ibid.
27 Ibid.
28 Ibid.
29 Ibid.

30 Ibid.
31 Ibid.
32 Ibid.
33 Ibid.
34 Ibid.
35 Ibid.
36 Ibid.
37 Ibid.
38 "Title IX and Sex Discrimination," Office for Civil Rights, U.S. Department of Education, https://www2.ed.gov/about/offices/list/ocr/docs/tix_dis.html.
39 Ibid.
40 Ibid.
41 Ibid.
42 Sandler, "Title IX."
43 Ibid.
44 Katrina J. Brown and Catherine Connolly, "The Role of Law in Promoting Women in Elite Athletics: An Examination of Four Nations," *International Review for the Sociology of Sport* 45, no. 1 (2010): 3–21.
45 Sandler, "Title IX."
46 Ibid.
47 Ibid.
48 Ken Miyamoto, "Why Screenwriters Should Embrace the Heroine's Journey," ScreenCraft, June 18, 2017, https://screencraft.org/2017/06/18/how-screenwriters-can-embrace-the-heroines-journey/.

Ruth Simmons

Carmen Twillie Ambar and Tyler Sloan

Background

Ruth Simmons's leadership style reflects her firm value system and upbringing in Houston, Texas, during the Jim Crow era. Her lengthy professional accomplishments include becoming the first African American president of an Ivy League institution as Brown University president from 2002 to 2008. During her tenure at Brown, Simmons formed the Slavery and Justice Committee—composed of faculty, students, and administrators—to investigate the university's relationship to the transatlantic slave trade. Despite the committee's final report earning international renown and Simmons's subsequent lauding as an intellectual pioneer, she would never list it as one of her most pivotal accomplishments at Brown. Instead, she names instituting a need-blind financial aid policy and the academic programs she helped build as the feats of which she is most proud.

Even with Simmons's modest take on initiating the Slavery and Justice Committee's work, the junctures during that four-year endeavor provide an ideal platform from which to extract universal lessons about leadership in the face of adversity. Her mantra is that universities hold a pivotal position in society to produce dispassionate, fact-based research in pursuit of challenging preexisting beliefs. As such, several moments throughout the Slavery and Justice Committee's history allow for specific insight into Simmons's leadership style and are thus the focus of this chapter: first, her initial decision to distance herself and take an extremely hands-off approach to the committee's work; next, her response to the committee's first draft of the report; and finally, Simmons's last look at the report and the way she presented it to the community at large.

These moments pose several major questions that illustrate the junctures (or the thrust of the leadership choice) for Ruth Simmons in pursuing the Slavery and Justice Commission: (1) How do you make the decision to pursue an issue? (2) How do you, through looking at an institution's history, try to redress past wrongs? (3) How do you balance personal leadership style with building the capacity for a group of people to join and contribute? Simmons's answers to these questions are what make her an ideal subject for this book and a stellar example of powerful women's leadership.

From these educational junctures, a portrait of Simmons as an intrepid leader and singular thinker emerges. In both her time at Brown and her previous position as president of Smith College, her professional record demonstrates a consistent commitment to uplifting those whose voices have been historically oppressed while facilitating open-minded dialogue about the nation's most pressing issues—a trait she credits to her childhood and upbringing. Though Simmons rejects the neatly packaged rags-to-riches narrative through which her life's story has been frequently told, understanding her background is imperative to understanding her choices as a leader.

Born July 3, 1945, as the youngest of twelve children, Simmons spent her earliest years in East Texas on the farm where her parents, Fannie and Isaac Stubblefield, the children of slaves, were sharecroppers. Too young to work in the field picking cotton with her siblings, Simmons instead found solace in books. When she was slightly older, Simmons's family moved to Houston's Fifth Ward, a deeply segregated area, in the thick of the Jim Crow era. In Houston, Simmons's father and mother found work in a factory and as a maid for white families, respectively. With encouragement and support from her parents and teachers, Simmons excelled in Houston's segregated public schools.[1] "This sense of myself came from my mother, who instilled in us very strong values about who we were," Simmons told the *New York Times* in 2011. "This was quite essential at the time I grew up, because in that environment, in the Jim Crow

South, everybody told you that you were worth nothing. . . . She would just constantly talk to us: Never think of yourself as being better than anybody else. Always think for yourself. Don't follow the crowd."[2]

After attending Phillis Wheatley High School, Simmons landed two scholarships that allowed her to attend Dillard University, a historically black college in New Orleans. Her junior year of college, however, she spent studying at Wellesley College, a prestigious women's college in Massachusetts. Simmons has often discussed this year as a formative moment in her education, saying that then president Margaret Clapp inspired her to reconsider her understanding of gender roles.

Simmons ultimately graduated summa cum laude from Dillard in 1967, which was only the beginning of a long list of academic achievements. Shortly after graduating, Simmons traveled to France on a Fulbright fellowship, where she pursued her passion for studying languages. Following her year at the Université de Lyon, she returned to the United States to continue her education—this time, as a PhD candidate at Harvard University studying Romance languages and literature. She earned her master's degree along the way to a PhD in 1973.

Not long after graduating from Harvard, Simmons returned to New Orleans for her first job as a French professor at the University of New Orleans, from 1973 to 1976. Her talents quickly elevated her to assistant dean of the College of Liberal Arts, a post she held until 1976. From there, she headed out west to California for six years.

At California State University, Riverside, Simmons served as an administrative coordinator for the National Endowment for the Humanities Liberal Studies project from 1977 to 1978. The following academic year, she became the acting director of international programs while simultaneously teaching as a visiting associate professor of Pan-African studies. In 1979, Simmons took an administrative job at the University of Southern California (USC), the first of many elite institutions where she would work.

Following her position as assistant dean of USC's graduate school from 1979 to 1982, Simmons was promoted to associate dean. She only stayed on for one more year in this post, though, leaving for

Princeton University in 1983, where she remained for seven years. Initially recruited as director of Princeton's Butler College, a residential college, Simmons became the acting director of the Afro-American studies program just two years later in 1985. From there, she eventually became the assistant dean of faculty and, subsequently, the associate dean. She is largely credited with raising the profile of the black studies program at Princeton. "Charged with strengthening the African-American Studies program, [Simmons] recruited Toni Morrison, Cornel West, and a number of other stars, making Princeton's program the most dazzling in the Ivy League," the *New Yorker* writes.[3]

In 1990, Simmons left Princeton to briefly serve as provost of Spelman College, the United States' oldest historically black women's college. Shortly thereafter, she found her way back to Princeton as the university's new provost, where she served from 1992 to 1995. In 1995, Simmons made history by being named the ninth president of Smith College, thereby becoming the first black educator to lead one of the nation's prestigious Northeastern institutions.[4] Preceding her appointment to Smith, Simmons was one of two finalists in Oberlin College's presidential search—a college that she considered to be more prepared than Smith for its first black leader.

An all-women's college in Massachusetts, Smith was not completely unfamiliar territory to Simmons. Still, the idea of taking the helm of such an institution was complex for her. She repeatedly pressed the college's trustees throughout the presidential search, asking them, "Is Smith ready for this?" in reference to the possibility of a black woman serving as Smith's president.

Ready or not, Simmons took the reins at Smith and immediately instituted changes to broaden its students' horizons. Among her many accomplishments at the institution were the creation of an engineering program (the first of its kind at a women's college in the United States), now known as the Picker Engineering Program; Meridians; the Poetry Center; and Praxis, the expansion of the faculty and redefinition of its workload.[5]

Discussions about racial representation at the college were also of the utmost importance to Simmons, but it wasn't just about talk. When Simmons arrived at Smith in 1995, the college had just 86 black students in its student body of 2,700.[6] By the time she left, Simmons had almost doubled minority student enrollment, bringing the enrollment of African American and Hispanic students from 7.1 percent in 1994 to 13.9 percent in 2000. She also led one of the most successful fundraising campaigns in the college's history, raising $300 million in the five years she spent at Smith, nearly doubling the endowment.[7]

Simmons maintains that women's colleges, unlike other "artificial barriers that separate higher education," are invaluable. Shortly after being appointed to Smith's presidency, she told the *New York Times*, "It's not true that all barriers to women have come down. We all imagine that someday we will live in a society that does not impede women. But will that happen in my lifetime? I doubt it. And so, for now, the best way to deal with it is to separate women so that they can achieve—especially in fields like physics, chemistry and economics."[8]

Her appointment was lauded by colleagues and renowned scholars, who cited her experiences at both Princeton and Spelman as integral to her ability to lead Smith. Frank L. Matthews, publisher of *Black Issues in Higher Education*, said of Simmons in 2004, "At Spelman, her role model was Johnnetta Cole, the president of Spelman; and from her she learned the practice of tough love—nurturing students with a realistic view of the problems that confront the black community. She believes that you get educated to serve the community. If she can convey that religion, then Smith will run circles around the other Ivy League schools."[9]

Five years after making history at Smith, Simmons went on to become the first African American president of an Ivy League university as the eighteenth president of Brown University on July 1, 2001. Known for its progressive student body, Brown is widely understood to be one of the most liberal colleges in the United States. Still, when Simmons decided to create the Steering Committee on Slavery and Justice to investigate Brown's founding in 1764 and its relationship to slavery, the committee was not met with unanimous acceptance.

The subject of paying reparations, a potential outcome from that investigation, was a hot theme in political debates occurring at

Brown in 2001. That year, there was widespread outrage when the school's newspaper, the *Brown Daily Herald*, published a full-page advertisement reading "Ten Reasons Why Reparations for Slavery Is a Bad Idea—and Racist Too."[10] Protesters who disagreed with the paper's decision to run the ad dumped the issues in the trash, formed human chains, and demanded the paper pay "reparations" by reallocating its advertising fee or reserving free advertising space to proponents of reparations.[11] And though reparations were a major point of conversation and media attention, they were hardly the committee's major focus.

Simmons's first speech to students as president included her support for the free expression of unpopular opinions, the grounds on which the paper defended its actions. The ad and its subsequent protests were later referred to as the "Horowitz Incident," named after conservative commentator David Horowitz, who paid for the ad.

Simmons's approach to forming the committee mirrored her support for free speech of unpopular opinions, reiterating that the group's mission would be carried out through a wide range of disciplines, opinions, and viewpoints. When she announced the committee's formation in 2004, Simmons wrote an op-ed for the *Boston Globe* to explain its purpose, describing it as "not about whether or how reparations should be paid. Rather, it will do the difficult work of scholarship, debate and civil discourse, demonstrating how difficult, uncomfortable and valuable this process can be."[12] She continued on to describe how understanding history is a vital tool for discovering the meaning of our past.

In her *Boston Globe* op-ed, Simmons also discussed the context in which she was presenting the commission. She said that public discourse in the United States is rife with one-sided arguments, name-calling, and finger-pointing, making it difficult to discuss serious ideas. She also acknowledged that many have claimed that universities exacerbate this issue, adding, "They complain that because of the current competitive climate, fundraising demands and diverse composition of campuses, faculty and administrators are unwilling to take on difficult questions that might result in the disaffection of any group."[13] She said, however, that the Slavery and Justice Committee would do exactly the opposite.

The commission was responsible for spending two years examining Brown's historic ties to slavery: "arrang[ing] seminars, courses and research projects examining the moral, legal and economic complexities of reparations and other means of redressing wrongs; and recommend[ing] whether and how the university should take responsibility for its connection to slavery."[14]

In today's context, Simmons's decision hardly seems like an aberration. Colleges across the country have recently been grappling with their own roles in slavery, with some, such as Georgetown University, implementing a version of reparations. But in 2003, when these conversations were happening at Brown, Simmons's undertaking was unprecedented. It elicited no outpouring of support from peer institutions. "While the move grabbed headlines, there wasn't a single peep from another university," James T. Campbell, the historian who led the Brown effort, recalled during one panel.[15]

Simmons never shied away from sharing her personal connections to slavery and her academic interest in reexamining its history in the United States. "It certainly didn't escape me, my own past in relationship to that," she said to the New York Times in 2004. "I sit here in my office beneath the portrait of people who lived at a different time and who saw the ownership of people in a different way. You can't sit in an office and face that every day unless you really want to know, unless you really want to understand this dichotomy."[16]

From the beginning of the project, Simmons insisted that she did not have a specific idea for what actions the committee would ultimately suggest. However, she did publicly say, in 2004, that she would be very disappointed if, at the end of the day, the committee returned with no recommendations for what Brown could or should do.[17] The committee returned in 2006 with a 107-page report called Slavery and Justice: Report of the Brown University Steering Committee on Slavery and Justice, which recommended "the institution to make amends by building a memorial, creating a center for the study of slavery and injustice, and increasing efforts to recruit minority students, particularly from Africa and the West Indies."[18]

Simmons's involvement throughout the writing process is not immediately clear in the primary sources that were collected for this research. It appears as if Simmons gave feedback at major milestones (in the beginning, after a completed first draft, before final report released, etc.) but that the work was mostly delegated to the committee she appointed. In February 2005, after the committee had been working for nearly a year, the group met with Simmons. In email correspondence following the meeting, the group was struck by how much information Simmons appeared to have versus how prepared the committee was.

The recommendations were a focal point throughout the writing process for both Simmons and the rest of the committee. As evinced in the notes and email exchanges between committee members, the group debated whether to take as bold a stance as possible or to frame the project as a piece of academic literature, ultimately choosing the former. The committee exhaustively discussed the scope and intentions of the report in addition to what it intended to accomplish. In February 2005, during the drafting process, committee member Ross Cheit posed the following question to the other members via email after meeting with Simmons:

> The question was posed to us last night: are we trying to
> write the most effective report possible or doing some kind of less
> strategic and more academic, if you will, endeavor? I don't think
> we actually have an answer, and I think that we need one. Being
> effective suggests, I think, being (1) unanimous on our recom-
> mendations and (2) what might be called strategically bold in our
> recommendations—that is, figuring out the boldest thing/s we can
> insist on without presenting a laundry list that can be dismissed as
> unrealistic. Being something more academic would likely foster and
> celebrate dissent, and might prefer the most ambitious and far-
> reaching suggestions over any effort to temper that enthusiasm
> by the realities of what might be possible.

The committee's internal correspondence reflects constant concerns about the charges of the project and how best to accomplish its mission. These concerns are seen most clearly in the emails and memorandums exchanged internally. Mostly, these worries centered on the underrepresentation of different enslaved communities and whether the claims were too far-reaching or too limited. Simmons's feedback after one of the later drafts focused on the language used in the recommendations and questioned the use of terms like *underrepresented minorities* and *historical complicity*, for their ambiguity. The group closely monitored feedback from the media and alumni after the report was published. Responses varied widely, from absolute condemnation of the group's efforts and mission (some criticism was based on misinformation about the project's purpose) to celebration of Brown's actions. The final report resulted in substantial progress on all its goals of creating a center for the study of slavery, recruiting more minority students, and establishing a memorial. However, the purpose of this chapter is not to focus on the results of the committee's work but rather to analyze the choice Simmons made to form the committee itself and to determine if there are lessons we can learn from Simmons's leadership choices generally around this matter.

Resolution

Lesson 1: How Do You Decide Which Issues to Pursue?

The research surrounding the Committee on Slavery and Justice took us through the archives at Brown University, where we reviewed primary committee documents, emails, and memorandums; interviews with committee members Brenda Allen (associate provost and director of Institutional Diversity [2003–2009]) and[19] James Campbell (chair of the committee and, at the time, associate professor of American civilization, Africana studies, and history);[20] and an interview with Ruth Simmons.

When assessing Simmons's presidency at Brown, it is very clear that one of her signature achievements, which she may be best known for in higher education and among the public, is indeed the Committee on Slavery and Justice. As she noted in our interview, it is the matter that she is most asked to speak about, particularly by organizations looking to respond to a complicated history.[21] Simmons has spoken at the United Nations, at corporations like Goldman Sachs, and at universities around the world on this aspect of her tenure at Brown. Despite outward praise for this work and its results, Simmons's view is that this is not her most important achievement. In fact, her perspective on this signature work is more nuanced and analytical: "It [felt] like the right decision. It [didn't] feel like a bold decision. I like to think, in universities, we're just constantly wrestling with trying to make the right decision, day after day. Sometimes they have weight and sometimes they don't; but it's very much the way I try to live my life. And that is to be nothing other than what I know how to be. And so, when you're making decisions, you do the same thing."

Looking back on her decision from today's perspective, it seems bolder than Simmons asserts. It also seems prescient given the number of institutions that are currently wrestling with their own histories regarding race and slavery (e.g., Georgetown University, Harvard, the University of Virginia).[22]

Simmons formed the Committee on Slavery and Justice more than a decade earlier than the more recent heightened discussions about the role that slavery has played in building colleges and universities in the United States. Perhaps the most important part of President Simmons's work on the committee, and the first juncture, was simply her decision to form it. One truism of all presidencies is that you only have a certain amount of political capital, and it is best to use it carefully and wisely. So one of our first questions in our research was simply, Why did Simmons believe that this project, one without much upside in terms of the typical measurements of presidential success (such as new academic program, stronger fundraising, increasing enrollment), was worth pursuing?

James Campbell gives some insight into this question. Campbell's view is that two issues converged that influenced Simmons's decision to form the committee.[23] The first was the conservative activist David Horowitz. As is now common lore, Horowitz's placement of the paid advertisement in the *Brown Daily Herald* that recounted the ten reasons why reparations for slavery was wrong created upheaval on Brown's campus. Many in the Brown community at that time viewed the advertisement as, at best, having racial overtones and, at worst, as outright racist propaganda.

This advertisement created controversy on Brown's campus even before Simmons was inaugurated. The placement of this advertisement meant that the campus was poised for a complex set of conversations about race. And yet the students' first reaction was to seek the removal of the ad. Campbell viewed the students' response—namely, their effort to suppress the speech conveyed by the advertisement—as the antithesis of Simmons's worldview and the second reason she formed the committee. Simmons felt that the students' response was not only wrongheaded but a fundamental threat to the values of a university.[24] Campbell describes Simmons's inaugural address as the best university speech he ever read, in part because she addressed this matter of diversity of perspectives on a college campus head-on.

While both of Campbell's points resonate as reasons Simmons might proceed with the commission, the decision was clearly risky. Although Simmons was a seasoned administrator and a well-regarded leader in higher education, many a presidency has been upended by less controversial topics. This was certainly not lost on Simmons. Her contemporaries were also concerned about the risk and believed that the project would ultimately damage her career. Simmons responded, "I remember when word first came out about us doing this work, I got a call from Nellie McKay, a prominent scholar, and she called me and told me I had lost my mind. And that's what all my colleagues were saying—that something had gone awry and I had lost all touch with reality because surely I must know that this would be the end of my presidency."

So why do it?

The important perspective here is Simmons's. Given how doubtful it was at the outset that the commission's work would one day be deemed an important measure of her success, Simmons was clear in her own mind about why pursuing the truth at Brown was important. The first was her view of universities and colleges as important instruments serving the public. She believed that the core work of a university was to demonstrate its value as a place of research and analysis on topics of historical significance. Simmons believes that universities' inability to do this work, particularly with respect to controversial topics, is one of the significant failures of higher education and one of the reasons for the public's declining trust in colleges and universities:

> I thought that universities have an obligation to the integrity of what they do, and it is at our peril that we abandon the processes [of research and analysis] that are well tested over time in delivering information to the public. . . . In recent decades, we've of course abandoned some of the things we've been doing as universities and we've suffered as a consequence. And so our public relations, for example, probably hurts us as much as it helps us. . . . Our inclination to always put the best face on everything we do instead of laying open for others what it is we do and why we do it—I think there's been a cost for that. And as a consequence, I think the public is more distrustful of what we say.

The second reason Simmons decided to form the committee is simple but profound: "Telling the truth does not sow discord. Telling lies sows discord." Simmons's view was that the pursuit of fully exploring Brown's role in the slave trade would show the college at its best. Simmons would not be deterred from telling the truth about Brown's past, and her belief in truth telling was informed by her sense of the public nature of universities and her commitment to demonstrating Brown's value and values. She felt that if the scholarship and research of the committee were carefully done (a factual analysis based on strong documentation), the project would place the university's core assets on display even if the truth was complicated and unflattering.

For a project that her colleagues had described as a harebrained quest that might cost Simmons her presidency, the Committee on Slavery and Justice and its results have now clearly become one of her signature achievements—one that offers many lessons on many levels. We began this section with the question of how you decide what initiatives to pursue. Simmons's criteria with respect to the committee give us some good lessons. This project, for her, was worth pursuing because it elevated and reflected the core mission of the institution. When we have the opportunity to publically display the core values of our institutions, even as it applies to controversial topics, we are at our best. And leaders are sometimes rewarded when they make decisions in which the truth is revealed in areas that have been unnecessarily masked, even when revealing the truth is risky. As Simmons reflects on the committee at Brown,

> One of the most beautiful things about the Brown process, which I think I may have said in my letter, was how good people felt afterward. . . . And one of the most meaningful things to me when I went on the road to alumni groups after it was published [was] to hear from alumni and to have them say it was the proudest moment for them as alums. . . . And that was before the document really took off, but right at the outset—to say how proud they were that we had told the story and so on. So as I say, you don't know how it's going to come out until it comes out.

Lesson 2: How Do You, through Looking at an Institution's History, Redress the Past?

Early on in Simmons's presidency, she was asked by some alumni whether there was any truth to the question of Brown being involved in the slave trade. Not having the answer at her fingertips, Simmons went to her public relations staff seeking documents that may have been published about Brown and the slave trade. The response she received was that there were no such documents because Brown University had not been involved in the transatlantic slave trade. Thereafter, Simmons went to the official record of the university and to the institution's official history, but at that time, there was no official story that included slavery in the university's history.

In the end, because of the research and analysis of the committee, we now know that this initial response from the public relations staff was off base. But what is even more surprising is that Brown's role in the slave trade was actually hidden in plain sight. The committee's work revealed a treasure trove of documents, including logs enumerating slaves on slave ships, that were commissioned by members of the Brown family, whose name the university bears. Moreover, it also became clear that not only had slaves built one of the oldest buildings on Brown's campus, but images depicting slave labor on campus and slave logs had been used as wallpaper in one of the campus buildings. As Simmons notes,

> People walked by it every day . . . and that's telling too because some effort clearly had been made to reveal this past because they had pictures—representations of slaves who had helped to build the oldest building on campus—and they had a representation of the log right in the entryway. People walk[ed] past it all the time with no idea about what it was. So you can put those things out, but unless you put it in some kind of context, people don't know what they're looking at. So even though all of that existed, people were still saying, "We have nothing whatsoever to do with slavery."

An important question for many leaders, and certainly for Simmons and the committee, was, How do you redress the past as you look at an institution's sometimes complicated and complex history? This is a question that many organizations and institutions face. Simmons's experience can be helpful in thinking about these leadership choices.

One can imagine that to determine how an institution might redress the ills of its past, one could choose to look only at the recommendations that the committee produced and analyze their value. There is no doubt that the broad recommendations of the committee to create a center for the study of slavery; to recruit more students of color, particularly those of African descent; and to establish a memorial are laudable outcomes and helped respond to and redress Brown's past.

But in terms of looking at leadership choices and those that make a difference, the more applicable analysis for our work is to look at the process itself to see what we can learn about institutional efforts to redress the past. One important factor that reveals itself after a review of the work of the committee and the interviews with Brenda Allen and James Campbell is the fact that Simmons did not have a specific idea or outcome that she expected from the committee's work. Brenda Allen indicated that the committee was fortunate that Simmons respected academics, the analytical process, and research and that the only thing she was required to do as the representative of the president's office was to hold the group's conversations to the highest intellectual and scholarly standards.[25] Simmons's only real requirement was what she said publicly—namely, that she would be disappointed if, at the end of the day, the committee returned with no recommendations for what Brown could or should do.[26]

This approach, an openness to a process of analysis free of any need for a defined outcome, is difficult for many leaders. Being willing to proceed in this way when the matter to be analyzed is controversial is truly rare. But Simmons was clear that she had no outcome in mind and no result that she was seeking, even though these were matters she certainly cared about a great deal. Simmons attributes the trust she had in a process in which the outcome was not predetermined to her experience and reputation:

> I have to also say, though, that as an experienced person with a long reputation, I think I was banking a lot on my reputation. You'd have to look pretty hard to find something that I've done that has not been very direct and very unexpurgated. So a lot of what I was thinking about was the fact that I didn't know how you could really know me and not know that I couldn't put together a sham process that would deliver something because I had a motive, an ulterior motive. So I think you learn as a leader over time to trust yourself and rely on everything you've done before. And I think the older I've gotten, the more I've relied on that.

This willingness to create a process that was open to a variety of results was an important part of the positive way that Simmons's efforts were ultimately received. This seems to be a window into the first lesson in how leaders might successfully redress the past as they look at an institution's history. Creating a process that was open to a variety of results was key to Simmons's success.

The second lesson in redressing the past was Simmons's effort to find a way to have a variety of voices be heard and to encourage all involved not to be myopic. Simmons's initial openness to a process with no defined outcome helped the committee focus on the highest level of intellectual inquiry. With intellectual inquiry as the motivating factor, the committee members could more easily suppress their personal views, thus allowing more space for opposing viewpoints to be heard. This second lesson made the exploration of the institution's past somewhat easier by giving the members a certain intellectual distance from such an emotionally charged subject.

Brenda Allen said as much in her interview. Allen believed that when discussing slavery and justice, there is often a tendency to revert to the personal while ignoring research. Allen felt that the topic before the committee was ripe for anecdotal and personal perspectives to invade the process. What the committee strove to do was to remove the personal from the conversation and take on the challenge from an intellectual point of view.[27]

This is the fundamental approach scholars must take to put personal feelings aside so that competing viewpoints can be explored, challenged, heard, debunked, or adopted. Ultimately, the committee members did not let their own personal agendas influence the intellectual rigor of the project. As the project developed, committee members got past individual passions and elevated themselves to a set of recommendations and ideas that respected all parties involved.[28] This approach—allowing a variety of viewpoints to be heard while muting personal perspectives and elevating rigorous intellectual inquiry—contributed to the successful effort by the committee to redress the institution's past.

The final lesson in Simmons's work of redressing the institution's problematic past is a lesson we learned in part before—namely, her view that the committee could not go wrong if its labors were clearly the work that universities do. This view of the centrality of the committee's efforts to the core mission of the institution was consistently established by Simmons in her conversations with the committee. Simmons understood that the committee was fearful of how their recommendations might be perceived by the campus community, alumni, and beyond. The committee's work not only was of interest to the campus but had been covered nationally, and all eyes and attention were on this committee. The committee was receiving hate mail regularly, and the attention was likely overwhelming. Despite this scrutiny, Simmons never wavered from her view that they could not go wrong if they simply did what universities do. Simmons believed that modeling what universities do through the vehicle of this committee's work was another way to insulate them from criticism while simultaneously redressing the past.[29]

Campbell suggests that Simmons's almost idealistic view of the role of universities is, in part, what drove her commitment to this project and ensured its success. Campbell, in recounting a conversation he had with Simmons, said that she understood, in the most substantive way, exactly what universities do. Universities do studies and research, create centers, provide opportunities for students, and create monuments.[30] As long as Brown was modeling what universities do, they would prevail; Campbell said Simmons had this insight from the beginning, and it proved correct.

As Campbell notes, the committee certainly had its difficulties, particularly in the early days and especially from the conservative media. However, once the report was published and it had modeled reflective, rigorous analysis and showed what a university could do and what a university was, the response was mostly positive.[31] Campbell knew that this was Simmons's vision from the start:

> It might have been the *New York Times*, but one of the editorials that kind of extolled the committee after the report came out and said, "You know, it's nice to have a university remind us what a university is." And she [Simmons] had that from the very beginning. It was, for me—and I hope you can feature this in some of what you're saying—it's fundamental. I think what drives her is a deep faith in the ideal of a university. It's quite an extraordinary idealism; a belief that universities—if they live according to the values they profess of open inquiry, civil dialogue, fearless interrogation of existing orthodoxy—can surprise us. And I think that's just her belief.[32]

Simmons was able to achieve something very difficult. Through the committee's good work, she was able to look successfully through Brown's complicated, racialized history and redress the past. Simmons continues to downplay the achievement, but she is aware that others around the world view her work in this regard as seminal. She says, "The emotion of doing something because it's right to do it—we forget how galvanizing it is. And although I don't consider it to be that pivotal, I know that other people do for their own reasons. Not for my reasons, for their own reasons. And I think I don't underestimate the importance of bringing this issue to the country and having so many disparate places do it. I went to Goldman Sachs and did a piece on it. It's been amazing how many different venues want to talk about this difficult issue but never knew that they could."

Simmons's decision to create the Committee on Slavery and Justice has certainly been hailed as a signature achievement of her presidency at Brown. Despite the potential consequences and the relatively limited value of the committee's work to the typical measures of presidential success, she chose to pursue the work nonetheless. Simmons's perspective was that the committee's efforts were in keeping with the institution's core work of researching and analyzing complex (and sometimes controversial) problems and also in keeping with the university's mission of serving the public good. Fundamentally, she thought it was simply the right thing to do. It was the essence of what a university can and should do: educate its students, faculty, staff, alumni, and by extension, the broader society by rigorously seeking and clearly telling the truth.

Simmons believed that the committee's process would ultimately guide Brown through its controversial history and allow the institution to look at its past and find a way to redress it. Simmons's approach was to broadly charge the committee to research and analyze the question of Brown's role in the transatlantic slave trade and then to take a hands-off approach. Simmons wanted the committee's work to be done in a way that did not produce a predetermined outcome. This approach and openness resulted in not only an outcome that was not predetermined; it also ensured that a variety of voices were heard, it encouraged the suppressing of personal and myopic views, and it elevated intellectual inquiry as a primary motivator. Moreover, Simmons felt strongly that the committee could withstand criticism of their efforts and their recommendations if they were dedicated to the work that universities do: sound, factually based research and rigorous analysis.

Simmons's career is marked by many firsts, but she was ahead of her time in so many other ways. Many institutions have complicated pasts with regard to race, slavery, and the transatlantic slave trade. Simmons met this issue head-on well before other institutions began doing this work and before she was pressured to do so at Brown. That took courage.

As with all leadership choices, however, hers must be seen in the context of her life and career. Ruth Simmons's thinking and actions were informed by her remarkable intellect, her deep experience, and her unshakable sense of self.

Simmons came into her presidency at Brown with experience as a professor, a dean, a provost, and a prior president. She is clear that if she had been younger, she surely would have handled this committee initiative differently. She would have been less patient and less understanding of the lack of clarity about the outcome at the outset. But after years in these roles, Simmons knew that the initial controversy did not predict the outcome and that controversy can oftentimes lead to brilliant results.

Simmons could also stand on her reputation. She had learned over time to trust herself and to rely on all the things she had done before to give her confidence in the way forward. She discovered over the course of her career that you do not lead by being overly concerned about the risk; this approach would be paralyzing because every decision is fraught with a list of potentially bad consequences. She has always led with the conviction of doing what is right and the belief that this approach will ultimately lead to what is best for the university. Simmons believes this approach, focusing on doing the right thing and helping people recognize that this is a leader's core motivation, will result in success even if the initiative fails. In Simmons's view, even if a risk is taken for the right reason and ends in failure, people will still find the effort ennobling.

Simmons had also come to trust herself and her leadership. She had a history of creating consultative processes that engaged people based not on their stature or their role but rather on their willingness to be a part of the process as an engaged participant with a desire to explore ideas, to question, and to develop a way forward.

Over time, she came to learn that there is just one blueprint for leadership or a checklist of things leaders must do to succeed. Leaders use their experience, background, intuition, and humanity to lead in the situations in which they find themselves. In her view, they discover that, at their best, they lead authentically simply by being the people who they are. When leaders operate from this perspective, they tend to take a stand to do the right thing and then act upon it. Simmons's view is that we all should remember this is what leadership calls for: doing the difficult thing when it needs to be done. She says, "[Leadership] calls on [you] to know your community needs and to serve that community well. It falls on you to express [and] to explain what it is you are doing in the context of the circumstances at hand. It calls for all those things. And not for you to consult the public relations persons about what the best course is, right? Or your lawyer. That's the thing that people are waiting for from university leadership. And in my view, to the extent that we don't forget that [leaders] will be much better off in the end."

Notes

1 Frances FitzGerald, "Peculiar Institutions," *New Yorker*, September 12, 2005.
2 Adam Bryant, "I Was Impossible, but then I Saw How to Lead," *New York Times*, December 3, 2011.
3 FitzGerald, "Peculiar Institutions."
4 William Honan, "Smith College Makes History in Naming Its Next President," *New York Times*, December 16, 1994.
5 "The Simmons Years," *NewsSmith*, last modified May 9, 2001, https://www .smith.edu/newssmith/NSSpro1/timeline.html.
6 Ibid.
7 "A Woman for All Seasons: Tributes to Ruth Simmons," *NewsSmith*, last modified May 9, 2001, https://www.smith.edu/newssmith/NSSpro1/tributes.html.
8 Honan, "Smith College Makes History."
9 Ibid.
10 David Horowitz, "Ten Reasons Why Reparations for Slavery Is a Bad Idea—and Racist Too," *Brown Daily Herald*, March 13, 2001.

11 Diane Jean Schemo, "Ad Intended to Stir Up Campuses More Than Succeeds in Its Mission," *New York Times*, March 21, 2001.

12 Ruth Simmons, "Slavery and Justice: We Seek to Discover the Meaning of Our Past," *Boston Globe*, April 28, 2004.

13 Ibid.

14 Pam Belluck, "Brown U. to Examine Debt to Slave Trade," *New York Times*, March 13, 2004.

15 Jennifer Schuessler, "Confronting Academia's Ties to Slavery," *New York Times*, March 5, 2017.

16 Belluck, "Brown U. to Examine Debt."

17 Ibid.

18 Brenda Allen et al., *Slavery and Justice: Report of the Brown University Steering Committee on Slavery and Justice* (Providence, R.I.: Brown University Office of Institutional Equity and Diversity, 2007), https://www.brown.edu/about/ administration/institutional-diversity/resources-initiatives/slavery-justice -report.

19 Brenda Allen, in discussion with the author, March 27, 2018. Allen was the associate provost and director of institution diversity from 2003 to 2009 at Brown University.

20 James Campbell, in discussion with the author, April 2, 2018. Campbell is the chair of the Slavery and Justice Committee and an associate professor of American civilization, African studies, and history.

21 Ruth Simmons, in discussion with the author, April 27, 2018. All direct quotes and statements are taken from this interview unless otherwise noted. Simmons was the president of Brown University from 2002 to 2008.

22 S. Smith and K. Ellis, "Shackled Legacy: History Shows Slavery Helped Build Many U.S. Colleges and Universities," September 4, 2017, https://www .apmreports.org/story/2017/09/04/shackled-legacy.

23 Campbell, discussion.

24 Ibid.

25 Allen, discussion.

26 Belluck, "Brown U. to Examine Debt."

27 Allen, discussion.

28 Ibid.

29 Campbell, discussion.

30 Ibid.

31 Ibid.

32 Ibid.

Nancy Cantor

An Insider with Outsider Values

Karen R. Lawrence

Nancy Cantor has served as president/chancellor of three universities: the University of Illinois at Urbana-Champaign (2001–2004); Syracuse University (2004–2013); and Rutgers University (2014–present). Before assuming these posts, she was the provost responsible for researching and helping prepare the University of Michigan's cases for affirmative action (*Grutter v. Bollinger* and *Gratz v. Bollinger*), which were presented before the Supreme Court. Each of her major administrative positions prepared her for the next, culminating in her present appointment at Rutgers. This third act was in some ways unpredictable. She was not searching for another chancellorship after stepping down from Syracuse. Yet Cantor feels the current match between chancellor and institution is the apotheosis of her career: "This is the place that is reinventing the American Dream."[1]

This case study of Cantor's leadership focuses less on a particular decision or crisis at one institution than on the way one woman leader seized opportunities to enhance access, opportunity, and social justice in the realm of American higher education. In a recent conversation, Cantor puts it this way: "These jobs are way too hard and way too complicated to do them if you are chasing things you don't believe in. To say it more affirmatively . . . you've got to do it because you are passionate about the things that you can affect." This study highlights issues at the intersection of gender, race, and social change in the career of a woman with a galvanizing vision of the American university, public and private, as a public good and site of social activism. It is a narrative of accomplishment and success as well as a story in which the concept of leadership is gradually decoupled from traditional ideas of power and prestige.

Background

Cantor grew up in a socially activist family. Her father was a labor organizer in the Midwest until the family moved to New York during the McCarthy era. By the time she was born, her parents were in what she calls more traditional careers. Her mother was a gerontologist and her father a lawyer, though remaining involved in social causes. As a self-described New York City kid, Cantor was involved in the arts in the city, training seriously in ballet from a young age. Although she never pursued her dream of dancing professionally, her belief in the centrality of the arts continued as core educational and social principles. She gravitated to Sarah Lawrence College, a liberal arts college outside Manhattan known for the creative and performing arts. At Sarah Lawrence, she found the first of a number of faculty mentors, Deborah Macmillan, a psychologist with whom she conducted experiments on time perception and who suggested that Cantor apply to Stanford for graduate school, the school she herself had attended.

Unlike Sarah Lawrence, a place where women were in the majority and held major leadership positions, women were scarce in the graduate program in mathematical psychology at Stanford. Although she found her niche with a second mentor, Guianese professor Ewart Thomas, she tells the story of an elevator encounter with a rather imperious cognitive psychology professor that set an unnerving tone for her graduate education. Between floors, he asked where she was from, and she said, "Sarah Lawrence." His response was, "We don't take girls from Sarah Lawrence." A year later, in a talk titled "The Law of Large Numbers," Cantor used this anecdote to make the point that although this professor came to respect her work, he viewed her as an exception rather than the rule.[2] Although proving a generalization wrong by example might have been rewarding at the time, the lesson learned in retrospect was that it would take large numbers rather than star students to effect real change in gender attitudes.

After switching from the graduate program in mathematical psychology to work with personality psychologist Walter Mischel at Stanford, Cantor entered a subfield that included both multiple senior women and opportunities to study theories and strategies for making social change. Her academic focus on the psychology of personality and social cognition helped her formulate a theory of personality that has infused her scholarship and administrative leadership ever since: personality as a mobile construction rather than a fixed or inherited one. She began to research how individuals are constrained by the prototypes or stereotypes that others project onto them, with the categories of race and gender being strong components. She explored the way stereotypes of individuals limit how others see them and how they see themselves. This work on personality and individual development broadened to the study of social change and the possibilities for envisioning a different world. Specifically, providing an alternative perspective within an institution—seeing things differently from the expected view—became, for Cantor, the hallmark of a bold kind of leadership.

Cantor describes this leadership stance as one of occupying a position as "an insider with outsider values" and credited this formulation to the scholar and activist Anita Hill, who first proposed it in a 2002 *New York Times* op-ed. In that important piece, Hill praised the courage of two women whistleblowers who used their insider status to expose and reform the insidious culture of two well-respected male-dominated organizations, Enron and the FBI.[3] What, exactly, does it mean to be an insider with outsider values; how has this stance marked the course of Cantor's career as an educational leader; and what have been some of its personal, as well as institutional, effects? Her work in leading institutional change from this position has involved a concomitant journey of personal transformation that has been sometimes rocky and even bruising, an instructive process upon which she has reflected with candor.

As she launched her academic career, Cantor was welcomed as an insider and encouraged by powerful male mentors at a number of prestigious institutions. She landed her first job in the psychology department at Princeton University, where there were very few women and even fewer women in positions of power. Here, the quality of Cantor's work was recognized with early tenure and a research sabbatical. She took her sabbatical at the University of Michigan, where she says she joined "a circle of very important women in my life that have all stayed together."[4] There, she also met Steven Brechin, a sociology professor and the man who would become her husband. Her two-year sabbatical from Princeton (1981–1983) led to a faculty appointment at Michigan in 1983, a position she held until 1991. She left Michigan only after the president of the university, Harold Shapiro, moved to Princeton to take on the presidency and asked Cantor to return to chair her previous department, which she did. In 1996, Michigan recruited her to the deanship at Horace H. Rackham School of Graduate Studies, a prestigious interdisciplinary school within the university. Nancy and Steve returned to Michigan, where both the reputation of the Rackham School and the support of other powerful women psychologists helped Cantor broaden the scope of her impact. One of the school's goals was to create a diverse graduate cohort that would lead to a diverse professoriate. The compelling interests of diversity and inclusion—for higher education and for society more generally—increasingly became a focus for Cantor as both an administrator and a scholar.

Cantor's drive and talent were recognized when Lee Bollinger became president of the institution and invited her to consider the position of provost. Both university president and provost were soon immersed in the issue of affirmative action. The lawsuits against the University of Michigan decided by the Supreme Court presented a unique opportunity to affect a key social issue that extended beyond any particular institution. Cantor's scholarship again informed her administrative work as she assumed responsibility for collecting compelling arguments for the educational benefits of diversity. The University of Michigan Law School's admission policy of affirmative action was upheld in 2003 in *Grutter v. Bollinger* (after Cantor had left the institution), with the majority of the court supporting the arguments presented for the educational benefits of a diverse student body achieved by considering race as a factor in admissions. (*Gratz v. Bollinger*, involving undergraduate admissions, was struck down as being too close to a quota system.) The work with Bollinger at Michigan solidified Cantor's role as an agent of social change, as she sought to widen the portals of her flagship university to include a more diverse student body. The insiders sought to ensure a more inclusive institution, arguing that the nation had a compelling interest in fostering diversity.[5] In a 2014 talk, Cantor reflected candidly on the limited focus of the arguments waged in the 1990s and early 2000s: "At Michigan, although the affirmative action cases were part of a larger national debate, the legal work was very much focused internally on the admissions practices of the institution and on those practices and processes of highly selective institutions like it."[6] As her more recent edited collection *Our Compelling Interests* demonstrates, her advocacy of diversity and its benefits in a civil society extend to increasingly wider academic and civic contexts.

Her very visible role in helping defend affirmative action at the University of Michigan prepared Cantor for further opportunities to make higher education more inclusive. When the University of Illinois at Urbana-Champaign sought candidates for chancellor, it seemed to be the perfect position in which Cantor could continue this work. During the interview process, she was convinced that the university and its board wanted a leader who would help unify the university and the community around questions of diversity. She knew this was a contentious issue at the time, which was publicly focused on the lightning-rod issue of the university's mascot, the Native American Chief Illiniwek. For over twenty years, this issue had been controversial and was debated on the campus, among the trustees, and outside the university in both the Illinois state legislature and the U.S. Department of Education. In 1995, the Department of Education ruled that the chief did not violate Native American students' civil rights. In 2001, believing she was hired to address the issue and with a clear sense that the board would back a change of this very visible symbol, Cantor accepted the job. What followed were three of the toughest years in her life and administrative career.

Resolution

When she began her job as chancellor at the University of Illinois at Urbana-Champaign, Cantor was a high-achieving, action-oriented leader who had achieved great success in her academic career. With a combination of hard work, talent, passion, and charisma, she had risen through the academic and administrative ranks at both private and selective public institutions. Despite the embedded gender bias at most universities, on the basis of her record and results, she was welcomed with open arms and open doors to positions of authority within these institutions. But she discovered an important lesson that is not always offered in studies of leadership: timing and fit are crucial factors in creating change. The work to transform flagship institutions into more diverse and inclusive organizations—even those where members of the board seem to support the initiative—can be stymied. She acknowledged the reality that "you have to be given permission to lead change from within."[7] Interactions with alumni of various institutions taught her this:

> A social psychologist who should have known better, how hard it
> is to combat the zero-sum intergroup friction that pervades our
> national discourse (whether around class, race, or immigration
> wars), especially when we collude in perpetuating the view that only
> a seat at the table of a few selective institutions will ensure suc-
> cess. At Illinois, when I tried to work on the inside to openly engage
> with these intergroup differences and historical enmities, around a
> decades-old and bitter controversy over the Native American mas-
> cot, Chief Illiniwek, I learned quickly that even as I might techni-
> cally be an insider, my outsider values marked me as different . . .
> and ultimately made it hard to lead change from within.[8]

There are many assumptions packed into this advice she gave the audience: the battles are particularly acrimonious when admission to the desired club is especially competitive, and this rancor is more virulent toward someone entering from the outside than a member of the culture. At Michigan and Princeton, her history as a collaborative leader helped her build trust as she sought to lead the institution; in her first chancellorship, fulfilling the mandate for which she thought she was hired, provoked bitter resistance.

Cantor's attempt to dismiss Chief Illiniwek from the playing fields of Illinois led to a particularly harsh public campaign that targeted her personally. As news reports from that time attest, a kind of public shaming was bought and paid for by some local residents in the form of dueling billboards representing the chief and the chancellor—he clothed in Illinois colors of orange and blue and she in blue and maize, the colors of the University of Michigan, her previous institution. The billboards were a constant and highly visible public reminder of the battle being waged on campus. Cantor says that for the first time, she internalized an idea she understood intellectually from social psychology: "The most important thing is that it really taught me, ironically, what I as a social psychologist should know, which is the power of context." Having a philosophy that you *can* change the world is sometimes not enough.[9]

Leadership studies often focus on decision points and strategies, particularly when analyzing the actions of strong leaders; this episode is an instructive reminder to analyze the very rhetoric of leadership and decision-making and to recognize that a leader is not the only one holding the cards. The power of context, in this case, meant that the decision Cantor sought was eventually recognized as the right one at Illinois and elsewhere, but at the time, it was unattainable.

After three years as chancellor at Illinois, when Cantor was approached by a search firm to consider the position of chancellor at Syracuse University, she says that both she and the University of Illinois were ready for a change.[10] She was attracted to Syracuse, she says, because it was an urban university that could potentially "embrace the thorough-going importance of diversity and engagement in the city." It had an active arts and theater scene—something she had cared about throughout her education—and the reputation of its Maxwell School of Citizenship and Public Affairs with its public-facing missions. "But the thing I actually liked about Syracuse," Cantor says, "was that it was a scruffy place . . . not uptight."

Capitalizing on what she learned about the power of symbols from the controversy surrounding Chief Illiniwek in Illinois, Cantor was able to continue her commitment to inclusivity for indigenous peoples from the beginning of her tenure at Syracuse. She invited Tadodaho Sidney Hill, chief of the Onondaga Nation, to represent the Haudenosaunee Confederacy at her 2004 inauguration and created the Haudenosaunee Promise Scholarship program in their honor at Syracuse.

Taking lessons learned from each successive institution and discovering how to change the outcome is an important sign of a flexible leader. During her administrative career, Cantor has learned to acknowledge—perhaps more than she had understood previously—the important consideration of the best time and place for making change as she sought to continue the struggle toward a more just and equitable society. In the wake of the Charlottesville violence in 2017, Cantor and Earl Lewis, president of the Mellon Foundation (and coeditor of *Our Compelling Interests*), wrote about what it means to both demonstrate courageous leadership and acknowledge the importance of local standards and circumstance. "Each community," they wrote, "deserves the right to ask how it squares history and memory. The answer won't be the same for every community, but leadership—courageous leadership—requires that leaders confront the issue head on."[11]

During her decade at Syracuse University, Cantor successfully led the institution to become an anchor institution in the urban community and to enhance its value as a public good, both in academic circles and for the residents of Syracuse. Through the extensive partnerships Cantor helped establish, the university began to give not only access to a different demographic of student but a stimulus to the very economic and social health of the city itself. In doing so, it provided a national model of access and opportunity for which she has been widely recognized. In an exit interview conducted in her office before leaving Syracuse, she was asked what decision at Syracuse would define her presidency. She answered, "To really conceptualize our institution as being engaged with the world, as being an anchor institution both locally and globally."[12]

The umbrella initiative Cantor created for this ambitious goal was named Scholarship in Action, a phrase that redefines the coin of the realm of a research institution—research and scholarship—to encompass civic responsibility and the goal of making an impact on society. This large initiative involved investing millions of dollars in the town-gown joint venture to revitalize the city. And by bringing the university's human resources (i.e., faculty expertise and talent) to bear on important societal issues affecting the urban community, the initiative also sought to broaden the conception of worthy work in the academy. The projects included connections and partnerships of all kinds—physical, intellectual, emotional, and symbolic.

Both the city's downtown and the relationship of city and campus were physically transformed during Cantor's time. Connective Corridor was created, a three-mile-long walking path that brought town and gown closer together, as well as a shuttle bus circuit linking the campus and the downtown area. A proponent of what she called "third spaces for universities and communities," shared physical spaces for collaboration, Cantor noted the particularly important role played by architects, designers, and artists in literally designing and implementing a civil infrastructure of connection. The Warehouse in downtown Syracuse, developed during her tenure by Mark Robbins, dean of architecture, as the architecture school's space physically embodied this idea of shared space by including space for a nonprofit organization, the Near Westside Initiative, connecting Syracuse faculty, staff, and students with neighborhood organizers, business leaders, and residents. Predating Nancy's arrival as chancellor, a downtown Center of Excellence for sustainability was embraced and strengthened by faculty in engineering and the sciences, areas that, as Cantor points out, care fervently about the natural and built world beyond the campus. Literal shared spaces were buttressed by administrative partnerships that she forged with the help of deans and provosts who shared her vision and were able to generate excitement and support among their faculties. Eric Spina, the university provost, helped her recruit and support faculty to lead in other academic areas, such as in the creation of the Biomaterials Institute, where cutting-edge research and public impact were a natural marriage. In speeches, interviews, and recollections, Cantor has continually emphasized that forging civic partnerships depends on having such team members. One key to the success of the project was a change in the academic system of reward, so the institution would justly recognize the scholarship of engagement with more than lip service. Interdisciplinary chancellors' grants were available for research that linked the university and the community. Cantor says she came to feel that not just collaborations but collaborative infrastructure were necessary to facilitate real change. Among her initiatives were helping bring the successful Imagining America project from its original home at the University of Michigan, fusing the connection between social justice work in the city and a modification of the reward system for publicly engaged scholarship.[13]

Many of the initiatives and programs at Syracuse were dedicated to enhancing access for a wider demographic of students, such as the collaboration with the national organization Say Yes to Education, providing in-school supports from kindergarten through twelfth grade and the promise of free college tuition to high school graduates from Syracuse public schools attending a wide array of partner colleges and universities. In 2008, the success of these efforts earned Cantor the Carnegie Corporation Academic Leadership Award, and Syracuse University became one of the first institutions to be classified as a university committed to community engagement, a distinction conferred by the Carnegie Foundation for the Advancement of Teaching. Cantor also found national resources to make science, technology, engineering, and mathematics (STEM) fields more accessible and welcoming to women, acquiring a National Science Foundation Advance Institutional Transformation Grant (with S. Bhatia, P. Brandes, K. Ruhlandt-Senge, J. Stanton, and Kal Alston) to support women STEM faculty at Syracuse.[14]

In looking back over these initiatives to make highly selective American institutions more welcoming to new student populations, Cantor believes not only that the university's research mission was expanded but that research was enhanced, not compromised, in the process. In bringing formerly considered outsiders under the tent of these universities and expanding their diversity, she believes excellence was enhanced. But Cantor's leadership has been controversial in some quarters, and in this area, she says she has learned lessons from hard knocks. In meeting the challenge of transforming higher education "to provide access and excellence for all our communities" (a phrase identifying the main topic of the Higher Education Resource Services [HERS] summit in 2014), she found how difficult it was for selective institutions to move from a model of prestige and exclusivity to understanding inclusion as a factor in strengthening quality. Her work on affirmative action at Michigan (a successful example of being at the right place at the right time) and her experiences at both Illinois and Syracuse have been funneled into a valuable but hard-won understanding: "At Syracuse, as successful as I genuinely feel we were through our kindergarten through twelve and city-wide engagement, in impacting the economy and quality of life within our rustbelt city/region, and in cultivating a new student body from metros around the country, the resistance of the 'old boys' (some of them who were girls) to the idea that diversity and excellence go together was fierce and played out in the pages of the *Chronicle*."[15] Faculty, particularly male faculty, accused her quite publicly of lowering the research reputation of the university with her vision of publicly engaged scholarship and her commitment to diversity. Adding fuel to this criticism among some faculty was the decision to exit, in 2011, from the prestigious Association of Academic Universities (AAU). She has said that she doubts people understood that the university under her predecessor was on probation with the AAU and that the move was better made by the university than the organization under the circumstances. In addition to this explanation, Cantor sees the move more philosophically—as a stance against kowtowing or believing in elite reward systems like rankings and bottom-line research dollars per se, independent of what you are doing. "Furthermore," she says, "the personal experience of this resistance, fueled by their identification with the elite and cloaked in the imprimatur of the chase for rankings, made me so much more appreciative of the institutions in our country, many of them community colleges and less elite publics, who persist in being committed to cultivating new talent and changing lives and communities."

Cantor has been quick to point out that the entrenched attachment to rankings and prestige was not merely a question of alienating some of the "old boys" as she pursued the more civic role of a research university; nevertheless, at least some of the disapproving discourse seems clearly gendered. Chandra Mohanty, professor of women and gender studies at Syracuse and a close friend and colleague of Cantor's, refers to the classic dual standard applied to leadership styles of men and women: "So while men are expected to be authoritative decision-makers, women are seen as overbearing when they make the same decisions."[16] Bold female leaders at the top are still a minority at American research universities, a fact that Mohanty sees as framing how some faculty react to the chancellor's courageous actions to carry out her vision of the anchor institution's responsibility to its urban community. In her current position as chancellor of Rutgers University, a position she did not seek but was convinced to explore based on her track record as a visionary leader, her outsider values are consistent with the mission of the university she heads. Again, in her address to the American Council on Education's Women's Network in 2014, Cantor candidly returned to the image of the outsider: "The bottom line, from my view, is to keep making our own rooms and to do it together"—a group of "insiders with outsider values!"[17] By both choice and necessity, she embraced this mantle as she assumed her new role in Newark.

And that brings us to her present position of university leadership, the chancellorship at Rutgers University, an institution that has fully welcomed the newest Americans for a very long time. Cantor was attracted to the city's long history of racial activism, regarding it as a place "that epitomizes both the struggles and the opportunities for social mobility in urban America."[18] This history included the 1967 Newark riots in the face of economic decline and inequity among the majority African American population of the city; the role of Amiri Baraka in those struggles and the election of his son, Ras, as mayor in 2013; and the initiatives now underway to spread equitable growth in the city by community leaders. In 2014, Cantor assumed the position as chancellor. In reflecting on why this position called to her, she emphasizes the inherently collaborative nature of both city and university that had developed there over a half century: "Fifty years ago, students took over Conklin Hall because there weren't enough black students. . . . What's amazing now is the collaboration across the city." What's going on, she says, is "collaboration on steroids, because there are so many different partners and issues and challenges." She regards her chancellorship as the culmination of her career of public engagement and her efforts to forge university-city partnerships. Rutgers is an urban research university with no racial or ethnic majority and a majority Pell-eligible student body and a tradition of embracing social mobility among first-generation students, students from New Jersey's large immigrant communities, and community college transfers. Again, Cantor and her colleagues have positioned Rutgers University as a leader in the work of urban revitalization and the achievement of social justice and equity. The university has just officially opened its Truth, Racial Healing, and Transformation Campus Center with community partners, one of ten colleges and universities in the United States participating in a comprehensive, national, and community-based initiative that was developed by the Association of American Colleges and Universities and funded by Newman's Own Foundation and the W. K. Kellogg Foundation. This initiative is dedicated to bringing about transformational and sustainable change that addresses the historic and contemporary effects of racism. The goal is nothing less than to "confront and dismantle the conscious and unconscious biases and misperceptions that exacerbate racial tension in America."[19] Cantor identifies her focus "on how to take that talent and intellectual capital [of the newest Americans] out into Newark and its metro region to collaborate (on education, economic development, strong-healthy communities, arts and culture) and be a full part of shaping its revival."[20] In another major collaborative initiative, called Hire.Buy.Live.Newark, Rutgers University and partner organizations from the public, private, and nonprofit sectors are establishing specific targets for employing more Newarkers, aiming to dramatically reduce poverty and unemployment and strengthen the city's economy by the beginning of the next decade.

It is clear that this view of the work of administration is anything but a view from within the ivory tower. Cantor says,

> I have never seen myself as a higher education administrator by vocation. What I see myself as is a public scholar. I'm not saying all presidents need to have that model. For me, it would be impossible to do these jobs if I didn't feel that my public voice and change-making proclivity couldn't at least be partly there. . . . Whether [in a] public or private institution, in this day and age, I think there's an enormous public responsibility. And the anchor institution work I have been doing for quite some time . . . is a centerpiece to what I think it means to be a responsible institution.

Her accomplishments and recognitions have established her as one of the leading proponents of higher education, whether public or private, as a public good, where institutions of higher learning become avenues of access to economic, social, and intellectual well-being. In addressing the long-term results of institutional change making, Cantor pointed out that much has changed at her former institution, Syracuse University, under her successor, and much remains in the DNA of the institution despite these changes. From her point of view, the fact that everybody gets deleted in different ways is not of great concern because she believes that the kind of leadership that depends on collaboration and multiple partners, as well as infrastructural initiatives, means that there has to be something that sticks.

In her recently published study *Women and Power: A Manifesto*, classicist and writer Mary Beard asserts that women must be "more reflective about what power is, what it is for, and how it is measured. To put it another way, if women are not perceived to be fully within the structures of power, surely it is power that we need to redefine rather than women?"[21] Beard goes on to explain what she means, a clarification that is germane to Cantor's career and outsider values: "You have to change the structure [of power]. That means thinking about power differently. It means decoupling it from public prestige. It means thinking collaboratively, about the power of followers, not just of leaders. It means, above all, thinking about power as an attribute or even a verb (to power), not as a possession. What I have in mind is the ability to be effective, to make a difference in the world, and the right to be taken seriously, together as much as individually."[22]

Cantor has achieved a truly effective record of making a difference as a leader in higher education, with an increasing awareness of how power must be redefined: with partners, collaboration, and the courage to both listen and keep going in implementing a vision. It's not a kind of leadership for the fainthearted.

Notes

1 Nancy Cantor, in discussion with the author, November 9, 2017. All direct quotes and statements are taken from this interview unless otherwise noted.

2 Nancy Cantor, "The Law of Large Numbers," speech, American Council on Education Women's Network, March 23, 2014.

3 Anita F. Hill, "Insider Women with Outsider Values," *New York Times*, June 6, 2002.

4 Pat Gurin, Hazel Markus, Abby Stewart, Susan McDonough, and Sarah Mangelsdorf, all former colleagues at Michigan and in Cantor's scholarly activism.

5 Years later, Nancy Cantor and her coeditor, Earl Lewis, president of the Mellon Foundation, used this phrase in the title of an important collection of essays on the salutary benefits of diversity to a prosperous democratic society. See Earl Lewis and Nancy Cantor, eds., *Our Compelling Interests: The Value of Diversity for Democracy and a Prosperous Society* (Princeton, N.J.: Princeton University Press, 2016).

6 Nancy Cantor, "Transforming Higher Education to Provide for Access and Excellence for All Our Communities," speech, Higher Education Resource Services Summit, April 10, 2014.

7 Ibid.

8 Ibid.

9 In fact, it was only in 2007 that the university announced the end of Chief Illiniwek as the official symbol of its athletic teams. Vernon Burton, president of the faculty senate, was quoted in *Inside Higher Ed*: "It's a long nightmare that has ended at last." The article continued, "The announcement from the university—rumored for months to be imminent—walked a fine line between blaming the National Collegiate Athletic Association for the shift and saying it was an independent decision. In 2005, the NCAA stunned Illinois and a group of other colleges by announcing that institutions that continued to use Native

American symbols or imagery in ways that were hostile to American Indians would be barred from being the hosts of postseason tournaments or from participating in NCAA championships if such images appeared on uniforms worn by athletes or others involved in athletics when they participated." Scott Jaschik, "More Than a Mascot," *Inside Higher Ed*, February 27, 2007.

10 Jaschik's article referenced Cantor's departure from the university and the problem the symbol presented to university leaders for years:

> Many faculty members believe that Nancy Cantor, who left the chancellor's position at Urbana-Champaign in 2004 after only three years in office, was in an untenable position at Illinois because of the chief issue. By the time she arrived, the chief issue was firmly in the control of the board and she did not speak out on the chief specifically. But Cantor is known for speaking regularly about the importance of inclusiveness and equity and outreach to minority students—values that were taken by some of the chief's supporters as some kind of disloyalty. Some of those supporters put up anti-Cantor billboards around town. (Cantor has attributed her departure not to the chief issue but to her desire to take the position as chancellor of Syracuse University.) (ibid.)

11 Earl Lewis and Nancy Cantor, "After Charlottesville," *Medium*, August 22, 2017.

12 Nancy Cantor, "Syracuse University Chancellor Nancy Cantor Defends Record in Exit Interview," interview by Dave Tobin, October 28, 2013, Syracuse .com, November 5, 2013, https://www.syracuse.com/news/2013/11/syracuse _university_chancellor_nancy_cantor_defends_record_in_exit_interview .html.

13 Imagining America (IA) was launched at a 1999 White House conference initiated by the White House Millennium Council, the University of Michigan, and the Woodrow Wilson National Fellowship Foundation. According to the program's website, the name Imagining America reflected the theme of the White House Millennium Council that focused on renewing participation in all walks of U.S. life: "Honor the Past—Imagine the Future." A consortium of colleges and universities developed from these seeds, with the University of Michigan as its first host campus and faculty member Julie Ellison as its founding director. In 2007, under Nancy Cantor's chancellorship, Syracuse became the consortium's next institutional host. Since 2017, the consortium's home has been the University of California, Davis.

14 The NSF grant was called "The Inclusive Connective Corridor: Social Networks and the ADVANCEment of Women STEM Faculty." See "Award Abstract #1008643," National Science Foundation, https://www.nsf.gov/awardsearch/ showAward?AWD_ID=1008643.

15 Cantor, "Transforming Higher Education."

16 Quoted in Marwa Eltagouri, "Bird by Bird: Nancy Cantor, Community Reflect on Her Tenure at Syracuse University," *Daily Orange*, December 4, 2013.

17 Cantor, "Law of Large Numbers."

18   Cantor, "Transforming Higher Education."
19   Office of the Chancellor press release, February 28, 2018, https://www.newark
     .rutgers.edu/news/media-advisory-ru-n-launches-truth-racial-healing-and
     -transformation-center-press-conference.
20   Cantor, "Law of Large Numbers."
21   Mary Beard, *Women and Power: A Manifesto* (New York: Liveright, 2017), 83.
22   Ibid., 87.

Nannerl Keohane and the Women's Initiative at Duke University

Patricia A. Pelfrey

Background

In the spring of 2002, Duke University president Nannerl Keohane convened a steering committee to examine the status of women at the university. Massachusetts Institute of Technology (MIT) had done an internal study on women faculty in its school of science a few years earlier that acknowledged that women, compared to men, were consistently paid less and had smaller laboratories and less research support. Other colleges and universities were beginning to follow MIT's example. What distinguished the Duke Women's Initiative was its ambition. Although the critical starting point of the analysis was extensive quantitative data, much of it new, the aim of the Women's Initiative was to answer a broader and more elusive question: What is it like to be a woman at Duke?

When the report appeared in September 2003, one answer drew national attention. A young undergraduate described the campus as a place where women felt enormous pressure to reflect an impossible ideal of "effortless perfection." The term was shorthand for a common experience, the Duke study emphasized, that living with "the expectation that one would be smart, accomplished, fit, beautiful, and popular, and that all this would happen without visible effort. This environment enforces fairly stringent norms on undergraduate women, who feel pressure to wear fashionable clothes . . . and to hide their intelligence in order to succeed with their male peers." The report cited the strong influence of sororities and fraternities in the prevalence of these peer-enforced expectations and the penalties imposed on those who did not conform. Such women students "often remove themselves from the social mainstream, whether voluntarily or not."[1]

"Effortless perfection" gave the Women's Initiative its most-quoted line. The dilemma it captured so well was just one aspect of the daily realities faced by women and documented by the report. Yet it went to the heart of a larger phenomenon that was neither unusual nor peculiar to Duke. "I felt there was a silence around women's issues," says steering committee member Susan Roth. "The Women's Initiative broke that silence." The *New York Times* noted the report's unusual scope: "There have been a number of studies in recent years that have examined women's standing in higher education—their numbers in the sciences for example, or in tenured faculty positions. But the Duke study, according to experts, is one of the first to look at the culture of women—graduate students, faculty members and staff as well as undergraduates—on campus."[2]

Had Keohane suggested this kind of critical self-examination when she arrived at Duke almost ten years earlier, it would have been met with instant suspicion. She was the first woman president in Duke University's history, a longtime champion of women's issues as well as a noted political theorist with a successful career as a faculty member at Stanford University and as president of Wellesley College. Nonetheless, there were some murmurings among the university community about the readiness of a former president of a small women's institution to lead a rising coeducational research university of more than ten thousand students. A member of the elite Association of American Universities since 1938, Duke had both high expectations and unrealized potential waiting to be developed.

Keohane knew she was seen as an ardent feminist at Duke and that her first task would be to establish herself as a leader in a new institutional culture and context. Her experience, she later recalled, helped her "understand how difficult it is to put women's issues at the forefront if you wanted to be taken seriously as a major player. I waited until I was already taken seriously and then used my prestige and clout to turn to women's issues."[3]

Nannerl Keohane entered Wellesley College in 1957 with a scholarship awarded to women students from west of the Mississippi. She had grown up in the South; had never been north of Washington, DC; and did not see herself as someone destined for an elite Northeastern college. Wellesley was a profoundly formative experience, not least because it was her first encounter with an institution in which women ran practically everything. Leadership by women was a long tradition at Wellesley. (In 1916, the student body was given an exceptional degree of control over student life, a rare phenomenon at the time.) She was uncertain about what to choose as a major until she took a political science class from Dante Germino, an inspiring teacher who kindled her interest in political theory. What appealed to her was its concern with things she cared deeply about: equality, justice, and liberty.

The college gave her a rich intellectual community and an outstanding education. The most memorable experience she took away from Wellesley, however, was something that happened in her sophomore year, soon after she had completed a course on the Bible. Sitting in Pendleton Hall, listening to a lecture on a biblical subject by an aggressively self-confident male theologian, she realized that one of his pronouncements was simply wrong. She hesitated, wondering if she would dare to offer a public contradiction. Then she raised her hand and did just that. He backfilled and harrumphed a bit but clearly had been forced to take her questioning seriously. "I knew then that I had the courage as a sophomore to get up at Wellesley and challenge authority, to set the record straight," she says. "And that Wellesley is a fine place to learn to be a leader."[4]

After graduating in 1961, Keohane spent two years at Oxford University on a Marshall Scholarship, awarded by the British government to intellectually accomplished American students with exceptional leadership promise. This was followed by graduate study at Yale University on a Sterling Fellowship. With her PhD in political science completed in 1967, Keohane began her career as a faculty member, first at the University of Pennsylvania and then at Swarthmore College.

In 1973, she accepted a faculty appointment in Stanford University's department of political science. A few years later, she joined a small group of women faculty who were considering questions that were relevant to feminism and their own professional lives: How would their academic disciplines be changed if women and women's issues were taken seriously? What would a curriculum in feminist studies look like? They did their work at one another's homes, sitting around a table or on the living room floor, in passionate discussions that often went on long into the night. As they argued over what could or should be done, one fundamental conviction became clear: they did not want any of their number to emerge as a leader of the rest. Women had had enough of hierarchical relationships; centuries of male leadership had served mostly to stifle women's voices and women's freedom to choose the direction of their own lives. This philosophy of community without leaders was key to establishing trust and mutual support in the movement's early days. Yet Keohane could not help but notice its costs. She had learned at Swarthmore, with its strong Quaker influence, about the strengths and drawbacks of consensus building as a way of organizing. Sisterhood was powerful, she concluded, but it would have been even more powerful in driving political and policy change had it been less reluctant to encourage women to lead.

Her deepening commitment to feminism was reflected in *Feminist Theory: A Critique of Ideology*, a 1982 collection of essays she coedited with Michelle Z. Rosaldo and Barbara C. Gelpi. "The construction of women's experience has never been adequate," she and Barbara Gelpi write in the book's foreword. "For this reason, feminist theory is fundamentally experiential." The task of feminist consciousness must be to create "a vision of an alternative way of living, in which individuals of both sexes can flourish in diverse ways, without restraints imposed by rigid and impersonal sex/gender roles."[5] It was an early expression of a conviction that theory, when done right, leads naturally to action.

In the late 1970s, women were in demand for provost and other administrative jobs. Keohane had a number of inquiries, including one from Wellesley. Her first impulse was to say no. She had served as chair of Stanford's academic senate but had no administrative experience. So when the search committee at Wellesley offered her the job, it brought on a genuine crisis of conscience. She was a dedicated feminist, and Wellesley was a feminist institution. Like other elite single-sex colleges in the sixties and seventies, Wellesley had considered going coeducational but ultimately did not. Keohane believed the college had half considered, half drifted its way into that decision. "I felt we were falling away from the women's college idea," she says. Wellesley offered the opportunity to show what a women's college could be at a pivotal moment for American feminism, which was moving from the victories of the previous two decades into the uncertainties of the 1980s. There was another and more immediately personal reason she ultimately decided to accept. "I'd been studying power all my life, and realized I wanted to know what it would be like to exercise it," she recalls. "Therefore, I said to myself, among all the reasons I am doing this and leaving Stanford—a place I love—is the desire to know power. Machiavelli thought those who observed princes understood power better than those who wielded it. I disagreed."[6] She took office as the college's president in 1981.

Toward the end of a successful twelve-year tenure, Keohane assumed she would return to teaching and research. Academic search committees began seeking her out again, however, including one representing Duke University in Durham, North Carolina. The chair was an old friend who was also the head of Williams College. He countered her initial doubts by insisting that the conventional wisdom was wrong: a college presidency was excellent preparation for a future university leader. Pondering the offer, Keohane realized that a dozen years of administration had given her mental muscles she would enjoy developing further. She had grown up in the South and welcomed the chance to go back. The challenge of leading Duke intrigued her. And she was young enough that teaching and research could wait.

Duke was a decentralized research university in which deans had considerable budgetary control and independence of action, a form of organization that has implications for the role of the president.

In one of her first speeches, she addressed this fact by noting that while universities are often likened to large ships, Duke was more like a flotilla, with the "deftness, imagination, [and] variety" this loose organization encourages. But a fleet of captains also needs an admiral—the president—responsible for setting the course and seeing that all the ships are headed on the same course. "In such a setting," she later wrote, "collaboration is essential—but so is leadership. A faculty critic of the administration at Duke once complained in a campus publication that 'the president thinks it's her job to set the agenda' for the university. I pled guilty as charged."[7]

As she began her administration in 1993, Keohane went to work on a long list of plans to clear the way for Duke's expansion and growth. "I came to Duke in 1973, and I saw the place change over the years," Susan Roth says. "Nan improved the sciences, the facilities, the faculty. Duke really came into its own during her tenure."[8] By 2002, Keohane had gained a reputation as an outstanding leader at Duke, especially in attracting financial support and also as one of the best university presidents of her generation.

The public announcement of the Women's Initiative, in what was to be her penultimate year in office, was no accident. Keohane was beginning to look toward the future and what remained to be done during her presidency. She had been thinking about gender equity at Duke for a long time and about the status of women in American society even longer.

The sixteen-member steering committee Keohane appointed in the spring of 2002, composed predominantly but not entirely of women, encompassed representatives from every constituency in the academic community, not just women faculty and students but women and some men from staff (including staff of the medical center), alumnae, even trustees. The last attempt to study the experience of Duke women, conducted in 1994–1995, noted the striking absence of information on the subject and recommended a concerted effort to collect comparative data over time. Some of that information was then available, and more was needed. Keohane charged the committee to produce a report that was substantive and empirical, using quantitative data from surveys and qualitative data from focus groups and interviews to give context to the

numbers. "She looked in all corners of the university to get information, and we found different things in every place," steering committee member Ann Brown says.[9]

By the numbers, progress was clear. In 2003, the percentage of
women at the graduate level studying the arts and sciences was
47 percent compared to 28 percent thirty years earlier. The propor-
tion of women candidates for advanced degrees had more than
doubled. Entering freshmen classes were almost evenly divided
between women and men. Women constituted more than half of
the university's professional, technical, and managerial staff and a
third of its senior administrators. These improvements, the report
noted, reflected changes in American society as a whole. But there
were also some disquieting signs. Aside from the school of medicine, the percentage of tenured and tenure-track women faculty
was 23 percent, and the rate of growth was slow. The report authors
note, "One of the most striking findings of this Report is that
the percentage of Duke assistant professors who are women has
remained stagnant in the past decade, while the number of full and
associate professors has grown less than we might have hoped. . . .
These data provide a striking contrast with the progress that has
been made and is being made in the admission and graduation of
students in each of the schools of the university."[10]

The path to an advanced degree at Duke was essentially the same
for men and women, the report concluded, but then their choices
begin to diverge. Fewer women were choosing to seek and achieve
faculty tenure or a position among the university's senior leadership. As the initiative found, "A small but not insignificant number of well-educated young women who might a decade ago have
assumed that their lives would include, in equal measure, professional success and nurturing a family, are now explicitly choosing
one or the other."[11]

Many women, whatever their status or responsibilities, said they
wanted more guidance and, in particular, more mentoring in making choices about the direction of their educational or working lives.
Better pay and working conditions, along with more flexibility in
work schedules, were at the top for staff employees. In the medical field, work-life balance was a driving concern. Childcare was a

major issue for just about everybody, and one of the initiative's early accomplishments was a sweeping adoption of family-friendly policies, including the major step of offering better and more generous options for childcare.

The single-most shocking revelation of the Women's Initiative involved undergraduate women as they progressed through their Duke education. In focus groups, they shared their persistent anxieties over appearance and performance, which left them fearful of taking risks—running for office and facing the possibility of failure, for example. The confidence gap women felt as freshmen was even wider by the time they reached their senior year. Undergraduate social life was dominated by what the report described as a hookup environment, in which men and women rarely went on conventional dates together but partied in groups that were often followed by casual sex. Typically, sexual conquests enhanced men students' reputations and sullied women's. The result was to define women downward.

Two opposing tensions emerged from the focus groups. Most women undergraduates accepted and, in fact, internalized the imperative to conform to strict norms of femininity while also striving for standards of academic achievement that have traditionally been associated with masculine performance. Some observers described this paradox as "daytime Duke" and "nighttime Duke": When women shared a classroom with men, they competed for high grades and high intellectual achievement. But when the two met socially, young women adopted a highly feminized appearance and behavior while young men remained much the same. As former provost Peter Lange puts it, "If you happened by a place where students were meeting up for a dance or some other evening social event, you couldn't help noticing that the women students were dressed to the nines and the men students' attire was casual in the extreme. It highlights the fact that there were two cultures interacting."[12]

Whatever else this dynamic meant, it clearly separated women from any sense of their own power and agency, a separation that was likely to follow them into life after college. What could a university do about a problem with deep roots in American society itself?

Keohane turned to Duke's history and her own experience in women's education for some clues. In 1930, the university had established a woman's college under the leadership of Dean Alice M. Baldwin, a history scholar with a doctorate from the University of Chicago. The original idea for the woman's college, classes for women separate from those for men, ultimately proved impractical. Instead, women students shared the same classes, faculty, and curriculum with men but had their own residences and dining arrangements, a separate and active student government, and virtually all the grounds of East Campus, the original site of Duke's forerunner institution, Trinity College, when it moved to Durham in 1892. (The college was renamed Duke University in 1924.) East Campus and the woman's college gave women students a psychological and physical space of their own, control over social standards and other dimensions of student life, and a powerful bond of community. It ended in 1972, when advocates for coeducation won over the trustees and the college merged with the larger university.

Yet thirty years later, in 2002, the women's college still had a strong resonance at Duke. Alumnae who had graduated decades earlier talked enthusiastically in focus groups about its success in producing strong women who left Duke believing in themselves and their future. What they took away from this college within a university was, in a word, confidence. Keohane saw the woman's college as a communal paving stone on which to build. The result was the Alice M. Baldwin Scholars Program. "We wanted to create a women's minicollege at Duke," says Donna Lisker, a member of the steering committee who also headed the campus women's center. "The Baldwin Scholars Program offered an all-women space that—unlike sorority life—is more about students' whole selves. We felt that undergraduate women at Duke did not always understand their own power, and the program is a way to help them realize and develop that power away from male ambivalence about women's roles and women's leadership."[13]

Baldwin Scholars receive four years of mentoring, seminars, and retreats; the opportunity to spend time living among other women; and opportunities for help in public speaking and paid internships.

The goal is to counter the paradigm of effortless perfection by cultivating the self-confidence and sense of autonomy that encourage young women to find their own norms, standards, and future possibilities. For many of them, the mutual support is itself a life-changing experience.

Keohane regards the program as a logical expression of Duke's commitment to equal treatment for men and women students alike:

When the decision was made to go coed, amid all the enthusiasm, there were some women students who worried that the woman's college and its traditions would be submerged in the larger university. Coeducation was supposed to be as good for women as it was for men. Through the Women's Initiative, we were learning a lot about the extent to which it hadn't turned out that way. In the 1960s and '70s, people thought coeducation was a better idea, but did they make the decision with women's interests in mind? This was one of the main motivations for me. It came down to an ethical commitment: to see that coeducation at Duke really is as good for women as it has been for men.

A truly coeducational university, she wrote in an introductory essay to the report on the Women's Initiative, would be one in which

- women and men were not assigned sex-stereotypical slots,
- women's voices would be clearly heard in the classroom and throughout the university,
- men did not act as sexual predators toward women classmates or employees,
- women and men alike would receive good counseling about career opportunities and be urged to set high standards for themselves,
- men would be encouraged to take more responsibility for home life and not seen as unserious about their jobs if they did so, and
- performance would be judged by results, not the number of hours worked at night or on weekends.

Finally, "Gender would not be irrelevant in such a world, nor sexual excitement and romance. But gender and sex would not spill over into all areas of life and make it impossible for men and women to live, work and study together as equals, and for women to flourish as human beings."[14]

Resolution

The Women's Initiative was a remarkably honest account of the status of women and a passionate commitment to cultural change at Duke University. It became a national model of how to address gender equity in higher education, resonating on campuses across the country not because the problems it described were novel but because they were so familiar. From concept to execution, the Women's Initiative was shaped by Keohane's decisions about its direction and goals. Here are a few of the useful perspectives it offers about leadership:

TIMING MATTERS. Keohane chose to act at the peak of her reputation, power, and experience in the community she led.

ORGANIZATION MATTERS. At the outset, she cast a wide net across the university, making sure that all the major constituencies of the Duke community were represented. The people she chose were experienced and collaborative. "When the agenda for the Women's Initiative was laid out, it was clear the president had decided that if we were going to do this, no one was going to be left out," steering committee member Larry Moneta notes.[15] Sheer size could have made the committee unwieldy and its discussions unfocused. Dividing it into subcommittees expected to agree on a common approach to data and procedures and then to report regularly at meetings of the entire group proved to be an efficient way of keeping the membership informed about findings and progress—and of reminding them of the need for action. In meetings and strategy sessions, Keohane held committee members to high standards and meticulous follow-up on findings and proposals.

TAKING ACTION MATTERS. The power to act on some issues did not need to await the release of the report. Most of the members Keohane appointed had the power to make decisions or to influence others who made decisions. The new childcare benefits, for example, were announced in the report not as recommendations for the future but as accomplishments already made. This allowed her to point to early results and generate a sense of immediacy and momentum.

DIVERSE OPINIONS MATTER. Opinions of all kinds received a hearing when the steering committee met, whatever the issue or however strong the disagreements. Keohane listened carefully and summarized skillfully. "She could take an idea someone had contributed and reflect an even better version back to them, clarifying the implications of what they'd proposed and making connections to other ideas and possibilities," steering committee member Judith White explains. "By the time she was finished, we all had a clearer vision of what we were trying to do."[16]

HIGH EXPECTATIONS MATTER. The president made it clear to the university community that the initiative was a high priority for her and that she expected results. This had ripple effects that were both direct and indirect. The school of medicine, for example, created the new position of assistant dean for women in medicine and science and began to expand from its single focus on programs about women's health to include programs on women's development and leadership in medicine and science. (Today these programs include men as well.) Keohane's highly visible sponsorship underscored the importance of taking gender into account throughout the university community. "Nan was a powerful, popular woman in a position of leadership," Ann Brown says. "It changes everything when you have a woman at the top and women at the table."[17]

EXPOSING PROBLEMS MATTERS. Keohane did not hesitate, as some university heads might, to publicize a study that in some instances reflected poorly on the institution. These included, for example, the problems created by the dominance of

fraternities in the social life of students,
the disrespect some staff employees encountered during the
workday, and the prevailing culture of unequal expectations
of women versus men. John Burness, who worked closely
with her for many years as the senior vice president for
public affairs and government relations, notes, "She was a
president who was willing to take on problems that carried
a lot of negative implications. Nan believed that universities
are places where society works out some of its most controversial issues; and, with luck, at least some of them can be
converted into a teachable moment."[18]

In the end, Keohane was a scholar-leader—someone who had
thought long and hard about the possibilities of leadership, including her own. "She had a view of individuals and institutions that
was influenced by her understanding as a political scientist," steering committee member Ellen Medearis explains.[19] Keohane herself
later wrote about her leadership style at Wellesley and Duke:

As a longtime faculty member, I used as my model a seminar in
which ideas are put on the table freely, working toward a better
understanding of the topic before the group. The value of this
approach is that all participants feel empowered to speak, and ideas
cumulate over the discussion. The disadvantage is that conflicts
among potential solutions are not brought out and the discussion
can become diffuse. Some of my officers felt we would have been
better served by a sharper confrontation of ideas. In this seminar
model, it is important to state the problem clearly at the start,
bring together the ideas at the end, and identify the decision that
has been made or the next steps in following up.[20]

In her role as an institutional leader responsible for adjudicat-
ing conflicts and promoting balance among competing power centers within the university, she did indeed operate like the admiral
of a flotilla, seeing that everyone was headed more or less in the
same direction and that stragglers were brought back into line.
As the leader of the Women's Initiative, she pursued a similar

goal in a different way, one for which the seminar is an apt model. Her approach relied on argument, evidence, criticism, the airing of ideas, and her own ability, thanks to her experience at the top, to step back, take a broad view of the issues, and make decisions.

The close of her tenure at Duke in 2004 gave her the leisure to reflect and write. While on sabbatical the following year at Stanford University's Center for Advanced Study in the Behavioral Sciences, she was invited to deliver a lecture at Harvard's Kennedy School of Government on a topic of her choice. That lecture—on leadership—became the germ of the book on power she had planned to write when she took the Wellesley job. Now her focus had shifted. "I backed into writing about leadership," she says. "Once I dove into the subject, I was hooked. I realized that power was no longer my real interest; leadership was where my gifts and experience would be better used."[21]

Thinking about Leadership, published in 2010, brought together Keohane's two professional lives as political theorist and academic leader. She explains, "[I wrote it] to clear away some of the underbrush that prevents us from seeing clearly what we are analyzing when we think about leadership, and to suggest some of the questions we need to answer if we are to understand leadership more fully." The book more than lives up to that ambition. It begins with a definition broad enough to encompass the basic similarities that underlie many different theories and types: "Leaders determine or clarify goals for a group of individuals and bring together the energies of members of that group to accomplish those goals."[22] From this premise, *Thinking about Leadership* draws on history, political theory, and practical experience to pin down a subject that often proves elusive. Her account is rich in examples of the theory and practice of leadership, from Plato's disquisitions on politics as an art to the internal struggles of Katharine Graham, lying awake at night worrying about whether she would ever prove adequate to lead the *Washington Post*.

The chapter on gender and leadership asks if gender makes a difference and concludes that it does. Yet Keohane also concludes, based on her own experience, that "the effects of organizational culture and the demands of institutional leadership outweigh any effects of gender. . . . I cherish the hope that, in the future, as more and more women provide leadership, individual women, like men, will simply be regarded as 'leaders,' not 'women leaders,' each with our own personal style of dealing with the particular challenges and opportunities leaders face."[23]

In 2005, Keohane was appointed the Laurance S. Rockefeller Visiting Professor of Distinguished Teaching at Princeton's Woodrow Wilson School and University Center for Human Values. In 2009, she was asked by Princeton president Shirley M. Tilghman to chair the Steering Committee on Undergraduate Women's Leadership.

The study was occasioned, first of all, by an institutional anniversary. In 2009, Princeton had been coeducational for forty years. It had produced women leaders from all walks of life, including two sitting women justices on the Supreme Court. Yet Princeton women were lagging behind men in winning the highest honors and postgraduate fellowships, even though women exceeded men's academic performance on average. Fewer women undergraduates were serving in top leadership posts, such as student body president or editor in chief of the college newspaper, than had been the case in the 1980s and 1990s. The decision to explore these anomalies arose out of a growing unease about what, if anything, they revealed about the experience and performance of young women at this Ivy League institution.

The report, completed in 2011, found several suggestive explanations for the disparities between men and women in the share of highest academic honors but did not come to a single or definitive conclusion. This question aside, the Duke and Princeton reports shared some striking parallels in their findings about women's undergraduate experience and expectations. Like their counterparts at Duke, women undergraduates at Princeton contributed valuable leadership in roles outside the spotlight (and some preferred it that way). In both instances, women undergraduates had been active and successful in leadership positions in student government and student organizations during the 1980s and 1990s, but that trend appeared to be in decline. And like their counterparts at Duke, women undergraduates reported pressures to meet social expectations about appearance and behavior that men did not. They also arrived at Princeton with a confidence deficit that expanded rather than shrank over their undergraduate years. "Women consistently undersell themselves," the report emphasized, "and sometimes make self-deprecating remarks in situations where men might stress their own accomplishments. This was described by one alumna as the 'intensity of self-effacement' to which women may be subject."[24]

Mentoring—the availability of role models, good advice, relationships with older students or faculty or alumnae—is a strong corrective for a tendency to engage in unrealistically low self-assessment. It was endorsed by both reports. The Princeton study underscored the value of *early* mentoring for women. As Keohane explains,

> In conversations with alumnae, mentoring was mentioned more than anything else as a crucial factor in helping people become leaders. It was quite striking. . . . When men talk about mentoring, they talk about somebody taking them on once they've got a post. They bring themselves to the attention of someone at their organization, and that person—usually a man—takes them under his wing, helps them learn the ropes, and sees it as his responsibility to help them flourish. In my experience, women are more likely to say that their whole decision to join an organization, try for a fellowship, or take a leadership position was influenced heavily by a mentor.[25]

There were some at Duke who felt the Women's Initiative did not go far enough or that an investment of more money for programs or an annual lecture would have reinforced its impact. Others considered it too little, too late, or insufficiently attentive to men's experiences at Duke (a subject Keohane wanted but was unable to pursue because of the many issues that crowded the initiative's agenda). Even if true, of course, these criticisms do not diminish either the force of its arguments or its influence on the continuing national conversation about women's issues. Its message that coeducation must embody real equality for women remains powerful and relevant, and the energy it released continues to work its way through the university community. As Ellen Medearis replied when asked about the future, "I think it can be organic, to some extent.

Someone has to watch the flowers bloom and see where the seeds go. But we must also make sure that, when young women come here as students, we are ready to listen—and act if necessary—when they say, 'This is what it means to be a woman at Duke.'"[26]

If undergraduate women are opting out, hesitating, or choosing not to lead, what are the consequences for them and for society? Why is it that women—who now outpace men in college and university enrollments and the award of advanced degrees—have yet to reach parity with men in leadership posts at colleges and universities? These questions are part of the larger issue raised at Duke and at Princeton: whether the weight of persistent, deep-rooted societal images and expectations discourages young women from aiming as high as their talents could take them. A fascinating puzzle is why, since the end of the 1990s, the participation of college and university women in leadership positions appears to have fallen off to some degree. Higher education has a responsibility to continue looking for the answers. The limitations in data and analyses, the inherent uncertainties attending outcomes, simply mean there is more work to be done.

Notes

1   Women's Initiative Steering Committee, *Women's Initiative Report* (Durham, N.C.: Duke Publications Group, 2003), 12, https://hdl.handle.net/10161/8410.

2   Sara Rimer, "Social Expectations Pressuring Women at Duke, Study Finds," *New York Times*, September 24, 2003.

3   Nannerl O. Keohane, *Higher Ground: Ethics and Leadership in the Modern University* (Durham, N.C.: Duke University Press, 2006), 198–199.

4   Nannerl O. Keohane, in discussion with the author, June 12, 2017.

5   Nannerl O. Keohane, Michelle Z. Rosaldo, and Barbara C. Gelpi, *Feminist Theory: A Critique of Ideology* (Chicago: University of Chicago Press, 1982), vii, x.

6   Nannerl O. Keohane, in discussion with the author, August 31, 2017.

7   Keohane, *Higher Ground*, 23–24.

8   Susan Roth, in discussion with the author, April 26, 2017.

9   Ann Brown, in discussion with the author, July 24, 2017.

10 Women's Initiative Steering Committee, *Women's Initiative Report*, 6.

11 Ibid., 4.

12 Peter Lange, in discussion with the author, August 9, 2017.

13 Donna Lisker, in discussion with the author, May 30, 2017.

14 Women's Initiative Steering Committee, *Women's Initiative Report*, 10.

15 Larry Moneta, in discussion with the author, May 18, 2017.

16 Judith White, in discussion with the author, September 14, 2017.

17 Brown, discussion.

18 John Burness, in discussion with the author, August 2, 2017.

19 Ellen Medearis, in discussion with the author, May 31, 2017.

20 Nannerl O. Keohane, *Thinking about Leadership* (Princeton, N.J.: Princeton University Press, 2010), 65.

21 Keohane, discussion, August 31, 2017.

22 Keohane, *Thinking about Leadership*, 224.

23 Ibid., 154.

24 Steering Committee on Undergraduate Women's Leadership, *Report of the Steering Committee on Undergraduate Women's Leadership*, Princeton University Reports, March 2011, http://wayback.archive-it.org/5151/20180104165453/http://www.princeton.edu/reports/2011/leadership/.

25 Caroline Kitchener, "How Princeton Is Trying to Get More Women to Be Student Leaders," *Atlantic*, July 6, 2017.

26 Medearis, discussion.

Molly Corbett Broad

Michele Ozumba

Background

When Molly Corbett Broad arrived at the University of North Carolina (UNC), she came home to find flowers, cakes, cookies, and welcome notes left at her front door from women she had yet to meet. The occasion, in 1997, was her appointment as the first woman president of this two-hundred-year-old public university. Indeed, Broad's appointment was a first in several categories—first woman, first non-North Carolinian, and first Catholic. Throughout her career, Broad demonstrated not only an infatuation with being a first but a determination to lead with values shaped largely by her family history. Her parents were both schoolteachers, and her mother, one of eighteen children, was the first in her family to go to college. She explains,

> The experience I've had was because both my mother and father were schoolteachers. That set the tone for everything that we did. My mother was a schoolteacher at a time when women could not be a teacher if they were married because they thought, of course, they'd leave to have children. But my mother was a schoolteacher, and my father was too. I had a cousin who I admired greatly. She attended Syracuse University, and I, of course, thought the best thing that could ever happen to me is if I could go to Syracuse University. I can remember looking in my father's eyes to ask him could I apply, and he said, "Molly, we can't afford to send you." "Oh, I know that, Daddy. But if I got a scholarship, would it be OK?" Long story short, I owe so much to Syracuse University. I got tuition,

room and board, books all provided. That's what made it possible for everything else that happened.[1]

Broad's journey to becoming president at UNC begins as a student at Syracuse University followed by senior administrative and executive positions at Syracuse University, the University of Arizona, and California State University. As a student at Syracuse, Broad recalls a seminal moment that defined her professional career path. After a blue-book exam in an economics course, the professor asked her to come to his office. "What are you going to major in, young lady?" he asked. She said she didn't know but was thinking about mathematics. In Broad's words, the professor replied, "I think you'd be a good student in economics. If you have any interest in that, I'm happy to support you." As an economics major, Broad went on to graduate Phi Beta Kappa in 1962 from the Maxwell School of Citizenship and Public Affairs at Syracuse University.

In 1963, her husband, Bob, received a job offer in Ohio. Broad enrolled in graduate school at Ohio State University, where she obtained a master's degree in economics. After three years in Ohio, her husband's job transferred them back to Syracuse. On returning to Syracuse, Broad served Syracuse University in several capacities that provided extraordinary experience in academic administration, as well as the intersection of politics and higher education. Between 1971 and 1985, she served as manager of the office of budget and planning, director of institutional research, and vice president for government and corporate relations.

In 1976, as vice president for government and corporate relations, Broad was sent to Albany, New York, to represent the university and learn about government relations. About this experience, Broad says, "What a life experience! It led to a remarkable change to the depth of my perception about how to be successful and how to achieve goals."

These executive opportunities came relatively early in Broad's career. Representing the university for government relations required her to stay in Albany during the week, returning to Syracuse on Thursday evenings. As a young wife and mother of two children,

Broad experienced very early in her career one of the biggest challenges many women confront when trying to balance a professional career and family life. She tells this story: "When I came home after doing this for a number of months, I had my briefcase and suitcase in my hands, trying to get the key to open the door. I just hit the doorbell with my elbow. My youngest son came to the door and said, 'Now don't tell me who you are. I know I've met you somewhere.' He started to run, and I ran after him. But message received."

As an economist, Broad often found herself as the only woman in the room, so it was unlikely that there was anyone around the table who could understand the double consciousness mothers carry with them to the office. She attributes her success during this time to her husband, who adapted his work life to accommodate hers, and to the support of her mother, who lived with them. Without this support, it would have been impossible for her to go off to Albany four days a week. "I laugh about it now," she says, "but when I think back to those days, as a woman, you wanted to be recognized in the work world. I had the silk bow ties. I had the pleated skirt, a jacket, and a blouse with bow tie trying to establish [myself] in the equivalent to the guys there."

In 1985, the University of Arizona recruited Broad to become their chief executive officer. Arizona was a public university spread over three campuses and, in the eyes of Broad, "wide open" in comparison to Syracuse. She served in this position until 1993, when she was tapped by California State University (CSU) to become senior vice-chancellor for administration and finance. After one year in this position, Broad advanced to executive vice-chancellor and chief operating officer. At CSU, Broad brought her experience and skills of navigating complex administration systems—especially at public universities, where knowing how to work effectively with state government is requisite. Once again, her experience at Syracuse representing the university in government relations continued to underpin her career.

While at Cal State, recruiters for the president's position at UNC called Broad several times, but she told them she loved what she was doing and so had to turn them down. As Broad recalls the occasion, the former governor of North Carolina and chair of the search committee, John Holshouser, also called Broad. She reports that he said, "I know you're not interested in this job, but we really would like to learn from people who have experience in managing these big systems. We'll meet you in Washington. Would you spend time with us?" So she went and tried to be helpful, answering questions that tapped her experience managing the twenty-three-campus system at Cal State. "The next thing I knew," she says, "Governor Holshouser was on the phone saying, 'Molly, you're one of three finalists to become the president of the University of North Carolina.'"

North Carolina is the second-largest economy after Florida among the twelve southeastern states.[2] In 1997, the state's economy was dominated by what has been called the "big three" industries of tobacco, textiles, and furniture (including lumber and paper). Much of the economic foundation of the big three in North Carolina was based on the availability of low-cost labor—labor that became available when agriculture was mechanized. By the time Broad came to lead UNC in 1997, North Carolina's economic engine shifted from agriculture and textile to new industries in technology, biomedical research, and banking. This meant a growing need for more skilled and higher-educated workers.[3] The dynamics of this socioeconomic transformation in the state influenced Broad's tenure at UNC.

Resolution

It became evident to Broad that for the state to continue its economic leadership, the demographic forecast for North Carolina had huge implications for the university's role in addressing the educational divide. The UNC system is comprised of sixteen campuses across the state: five historically black universities and one historically Native American university. Broad's ability to examine complex systems and distill the multiple layers of inputs and outcomes meant that UNC had a large role to play in propelling the state's future growth. With this view of UNC as not only integral to higher education but also essential to North Carolina's economic health, Broad states, "We want our outreach mission to mean transforming the economy of North Carolina so that its citizens can be prosperous in a global economy—an economy that looks very different than the economy that made North Carolina strong and prosperous in the second half of the twentieth century."[4]

As president, Broad commissioned an engineering study that examined the status of all sixteen campuses. This report, along with projections on the population growth among college-age youth, revealed wide disparities across the campus system in terms of enrollment, capacity, and infrastructure investments. UNC projected a 31 percent increase in enrollment at the university level and a 33 percent increase in community colleges.[5] The findings in the study led Broad to create the Focused Growth Initiative. *Focused growth* meant that based on a thorough assessment of each of the sixteen campuses, investments would be made to ensure the UNC system could absorb the anticipated growth in enrollment. As Broad related, the analysis concluded that it would take $6 billion to accomplish the plan, so she took her case to the North Carolina legislature, where she was met with a House and Senate that could not agree on the terms of the bill. According to President Broad, "This was on the verge of becoming 'Molly's Folly.'" Nevertheless, with her expertise in strategizing and figuring out multiple pathways to success, Broad decided to go back a year later and request half of the money; she would raise the remaining $3 billion through direct-cost recovery.

The study that produced the Focused Growth Initiative provided hard evidence of the need for an audacious plan of action. Broad would need state congressional support to overcome resistance to her so-called folly. And she would need to build a relationship with U.S. Senator Jesse Helms. She built that relationship with Helms based on respect. Despite major philosophical differences, Broad was able to overcome initial resistance and secure support from Senator Helms. She was also able to show state treasury officials that the bond would not adversely affect the state's financial reputation and that no tax hike would be needed.

Subsequently, Helms invited the entire North Carolina legislature to a meeting in Washington, DC. Every member of the state senate and house attended. This was unprecedented in the state's history. As chair of the Senate Foreign Relations Committee,

Senator Helms hosted them over lunch in the ornate International Room in the senate. As Broad related, he opened the meeting by saying, "I'm sure you're all wondering why it is that I have invited you to come here. I think we ought to support Molly's bonds."

Helms's enthusiastic support was essential but not sufficient. In the months following that dramatic meeting, Broad exercised extraordinary leadership grounded in her strong belief "in the strength of a strategy that collects and combines, rather than divides and conquers."[6]

What was different in her second approach to securing the state bonds? In addition to lowering the request from $6 billion to $3 billion in bonds, Broad used relational and invitational leadership skills to secure the largest state bond measure for higher education in the history of the United States. Advocacy for the referendum was not limited to the state capitol. The bond measure was much more than abstract bureaucratic business. The campaign made it personal by tapping into shared aspirational values for education and economic security. The bond included revenue for community colleges as well, deepening the need for support at the local level. To build support, Broad and H. Martin Lancaster, the state's community college leader, crisscrossed the state.[7]

Media and elected officials were invited to university and community colleges across the state to see the situation firsthand. A UNC television program reported the following scenes:

> Some East Carolina University students take classes on a loading dock. Fayetteville State University has students living in a hotel and worrying about transportation to campus. UNC Charlotte has a cap on enrollment because there is no room for more students. These are not isolated cases. Campuses throughout the UNC system daily hold classes in outmoded, deteriorating, potentially dangerous buildings. From science labs to residence halls, the university system's infrastructure is in great need; and, so far, no long-term solution has been found. The Klein Report, a recent facilities study, found $6.9 billion in repair and renovation needs for the system's sixteen campuses. Meanwhile, UNC is bracing to accommodate an additional fifty thousand students by the year 2008.[8]

Faculty members were deployed to barbershops and hair salons to engage families and workers in the campaign. The disparities were greater for the five historically African American campuses, but with the goal of raising everyone to the same level of functionality, African American legislators got on board in support of the bond initiative. In November 2000, just three years into her tenure, the $3 million bond referendum passed in all one hundred counties, and 73 percent of voters approved the measure. Over the next five years, $2.5 billion would go to the sixteen campuses in the UNC system and $6 million to the state's fifty-nine community colleges.[9]

This was an extraordinary achievement on many levels: fiscal, political, social, and administrative. In a state with a history of racial segregation; a large rural, working-class population; and an economy in flux due to the globalization of a cheap labor force, President Broad was able to successfully mobilize a statewide campaign that brought African American state officials and Senator Jesse Helms to the same side of an issue: increasing educational opportunities for all North Carolinians. The $3 billion in funds for system-wide capital improvements had a ripple effect that not only improved the university's physical plant but can be directly linked to achieving the desired outcome: giving UNC the capacity to meet the growing enrollment demand. Between 2001 and 2004, enrollment increased by 12 percent.[10]

Broad took on several difficult controversial political issues but came out a winner in the most explosive one: giving the university authority on setting student tuition. When her first effort to secure $6 billion in bonds failed at the general assembly, Broad proposed a $100 student fee. This levy was unprecedented in UNC's history, and student protests led to this measure being dropped.[11] The North Carolina state constitution mandated that tuition be as low as possible. Decisions on tuition increases were made by lawmakers, not the UNC board of governors. Broad was of the opinion that this was not adequate for such a large university system. Like the engineering study, she undertook a comprehensive tuition study for the entire university system and, despite protests by many students, succeeded in negotiating several tuition increases in the early 2000s.[12]

The other potential land mine was affirmative action. As president, Broad was transparent in undertaking a public review of UNC's admissions policies in 1997 and 1998, during a time when affirmative action admissions practices were under increasing attack in legal and political circles. The purpose of the review was not to eliminate affirmative action criteria. Rather, it was to ensure that admissions and financial aid policies were well defined and unambiguous. This was not popular among students, but again, results proved the integrity of her leadership. By the time Broad stepped down as UNC president in 2007, minority enrollment at UNC had grown at more than double the rate of the overall student body.[13] As a public university, accomplishing these results required astute leadership with a deep understanding of the multiple levels of influence across the entire state. Broad was able to gain legislative support, build public will across a politically diverse state, and harness the support of sixteen chancellors as well as faculty and staff at each of the university campuses.

In recognition of her record of achievement over her eight-year term as president, in 2006, Broad received the University Award, the highest honor given by the UNC board of governors.[14]

Broad's prominent higher education experience and expertise, along with her skills in building coalitions among diverse constituencies, made her next professional move a perfect fit. The American Council on Education (ACE) is the largest higher education association in the United States. As an umbrella organization, ACE represents higher education associations on policy issues that come before Congress and the courts. In 2008, Broad was named the new president of ACE. She was the first woman to lead the one-hundred-year-old organization. Broad brought to this position a track record of success leading major public and private university systems, as well as political skills in negotiating and building collaborations that propelled major initiatives.

At the time of her appointment, higher education was facing tremendous challenges: rising tuition costs, efforts to increase federal regulation of the sector, and persistent questioning and debates in the media about the value of liberal arts education. The traditional college structure of ivory tower campuses and lecture halls was not immune to the growing influence of technology. The value of education was increasingly being measured by the earning power of graduates, a metric that, by definition, made majors in science, technology, and engineering seem the surest pathways to economic security. Innovation can often be experienced as disruption.

Broad's tenure at ACE was largely defined by her focus on technological innovation in higher education. This was seen by some as a radical departure from the organization's tradition of lobbying and policy development. With support from the Bill and Melinda Gates Foundation, ACE embarked on a collaboration with three companies that had platforms for massive online open courses (MOOCs). ACE's role was to assess the quality of courses offered and recommend those deemed credit worthy.[15]

After recommending the approval credits for five MOOCs, ACE came under criticism from within the higher education sector. An article in *Inside Higher Ed* featured some higher education leaders urging a slowdown of embracing MOOCs. Carol Geary Schneider, the head of the Association of American Colleges and Universities, is quoted as saying, "It would be a tragedy if you substituted MOOCs in their current form for regular courses. But it would be a creative breakthrough if you take advantage of MOOCs and other forms of online coverage to make more space and more time for students to apply concepts and methods appropriate to their field to real problems."[16]

In response to the hype around MOOCs, *Inside Higher Ed* published an essay by Broad in which she defended ACE's engagement with MOOCs. She writes, "This is a good time for all of us in higher education to take a step back and study the disruptive potential of MOOCs and other innovations. The American Council on Education, for instance, has an ongoing and wide-ranging research and evaluation effort to examine the academic potential of MOOCs and attempt to answer questions about whether they can help support degree completion, deepen college curriculums and increase learning productivity."[17]

She goes further to assert that this role is consistent with what has occurred historically:

It has been well publicized that one aspect of ACE's MOOC evaluation and research initiative is to review some specific MOOCs for potential college credit recommendations. So far, in fact, we have determined that eleven such courses across three major MOOC platforms met criteria for credit recommendations. . . . But what may be less well known is that reviewing MOOCs for credit recommendations involves the same work ACE has been successfully undertaking for many years to evaluate learning that takes place outside traditional degree programs. And faculty should keep in mind that it is their colleagues who are responsible for carrying out these reviews.[18]

Demonstrating her ability to frame big ideas in ways that make them practical and personal, Broad's essay asserts, "The promise of MOOCs remains an open question, but it's clear that online learning overall will play an increasingly important role as the higher education community works to serve millions of adult learners and help our country meet the goal of boosting the number of Americans with a post-secondary degree, certificate, or credential. About two-thirds of American college students now are post-traditional learners whose pursuit of additional knowledge and skill is interlaced with time commitments to jobs and family responsibilities."[19]

Much like her eight-year tenure as president of UNC, Broad's time at ACE reflects the same visionary leadership. She anticipated the increasing role of technology in higher education and forged ahead with innovative research on how educators could best adapt to the changing demographics of college students. With the numbers of traditional students on the decline, she recognized the new market of millions of adult learners who will need to earn a college degree while working and raising families. In the face of skepticism, Broad responded with a rational, articulate essay that made clear that embracing technology would not replace the traditional campus experience but rather create opportunities for diversifying the student body based on changes in the marketplace. Again, her ability to distill complex systems down to practical applications played a key role in her success at ACE. In Broad's own words, "I think the transformation of how higher education is delivered and how faculty members support, advise, and guide learners is going to be critical to a significant segment of colleges and universities . . . it is vital that we find ways, very different ways no doubt, to make it possible for individuals to get a job, or to keep a job, or to get a better job."[20]

Throughout Broad's career, her leadership has been defined as participatory, inclusive, and invitational. At each juncture in executive office, she was able to bring her vision for transformative initiatives to reality by building relationships, seeking strategic partnerships, and giving space for others to participate in decision-making. As the example at UNC with the controversy over student fees demonstrates, she also was not afraid to change course in the face of opposition. Her leadership was not about personal victories. Rather, it was about using her capacity to produce outcomes that resulted in improved systems.

Broad talks about her time on the Blue Ribbon Commission on Higher Education when she was the dean of the Maxwell School at Syracuse University, which allowed her to see how policy can intersect with politics: "It showed me that when you're successful at developing such a policy strategy that is also politically smart, you can really change the policy direction of an institution or even a state."[21]

Broad's approach to leadership in higher education was undoubt-edly informed by values shaped by her parents as schoolteachers and by her immigrant grandparents, who, without much formal education, raised eighteen children. Although she attributes much of her success to luck and the support of amazing mentors through-out her career, it is quite evident that Broad possesses exceptional skill and brilliance. As the first woman to head UNC and ACE, two institutions with a combined three-hundred-year history, Molly Corbett Broad is seen as a pioneering woman whose intellectual gifts, visionary leadership, and ability to inspire others will leave an enduring legacy in the higher education sector for decades to come.

Notes

1 Molly Corbett Broad, in discussion with the author, April 2018. All direct quotes and statements are taken from this interview unless otherwise noted.

2 UNC Carolina Population Center, "Carolina Economic Data," *Carolina Demography* (blog), January 15, 2015. This website is no longer extant.

3 Michael L. Walden, *Major Trends Facing North Carolina: Implications for Workforce Development* (Raleigh: North Carolina State University Press, 2007).

4 Francis L. Lawrence, *Leadership in Higher Education* (New Brunswick, N.J.: Transactional, 2011).

5 Jeffrey Selingo, "N. C. Passes Huge Bond Measure," *Chronicle of Higher Education*, November 17, 2000.

6 University of North Carolina at Chapel Hill, *A Building Crisis*, UNC-TV, May 3, 2000, http://gazette.unc.edu/archives/00may10/file.30.html.

7 Kelly Field, "American Council on Education Names Molly Broad as President," *Chronicle of Higher Education*, January 16, 2008.

8 University of North Carolina at Chapel Hill, *Building Crisis*.

9 Walden, *Major Trends*.

10 Betsy E. Brown and Robert L. Clark, *North Carolina's Commitment to Higher Education: Access and Affordability* (Providence, R.I.: Brown University Press, 2005).

11 Jeffrey Selingo, "News Analysis: ACE's New President Faces Challenging Terrain," *Chronicle of Higher Education*, January 17, 2008.

12 Patrick Healy, "A Modernizer Sets a New Course at UNC," *Chronicle of Higher Education*, April 30, 1999.

13 John O'Brian, "A Joyful Series of Breakthroughs: An Interview with Molly Broad," *Educause Review*, November/December 2017.

14 B. A. Robinson, "Molly and Bob Broad Honored for Service to Higher Education," University of North Carolina press release, November 10, 2006.

15 Sara Goldrick-Rab, "The Higher-Education Lobby Comes to Madison," *Chronicle of Higher Education*, February 20, 2013.

16 Ry Rivard, "Higher Education Leaders Urge Slow Down on MOOCs," *Inside Higher Ed*, July 7, 2013.

17 Molly Corbett Broad, "Beyond Skepticism," *Inside Higher Ed*, September 17, 2013.

18 Ibid.

19 Ibid.

20 Molly Broad, "A Joyful Series of Breakthroughs," interview by John O'Brian, *Education Review*, November–December 2017.

21 Lawrence, *Leadership in Higher Education*.

Reimagining Women's Education

Jill Ker Conway, Smith College, and the Ada Comstock Scholars Program

Susan C. Bourque

Background

From the perspective of the twenty-first century, it is difficult to imagine the excitement that gripped the Smith College campus when its first woman president was inaugurated in October 1975. Today, it is no longer earth-shattering to find women leading America's great public and private universities and that educating women is recognized as an essential part of social and economic development. But in 1975, that was not the case. The news that after one hundred years of educating women, the Smith College trustees had finally selected a woman, Jill Ker Conway, to lead the institution was a very big story.[1]

Jill Ker Conway was raised in the outback of Australia on a sheep ranch and educated by a correspondence course until she was eleven. Her recently widowed mother moved the family to Sydney and worked several jobs to find the funds to send her to an excellent private girls' school, Abbotsleigh. From Abbotsleigh, Conway moved on to the University of Sydney, where she won every academic honor but, upon graduation, was denied a place in the Australian Foreign Service (while male classmates with lesser records became officers). Frustrated with the stultifying sexism of Australian society in the 1950s, she won a fellowship to Harvard and completed a doctorate in American history. At Harvard, she met and married John Conway, a Canadian history professor and master of Leverett House. She and John moved to Canada, where she took a teaching post at the University of Toronto. Eventually, she entered the university administration and became a vice president, prior to her appointment to the presidency at Smith.[2]

Conway's appointment in 1975 was met with a range of responses. The students were ecstatic and soon took to chanting, "Jill, Jill, Jill," and stomping their feet in approval when they sighted her at the finale of the academic procession. The younger feminists on the faculty, although more subdued in their responses, shared an equal amount of enthusiasm. The much larger group of older, more established faculty members—both men and women—were more hesitant, wondering what was in store for the college under this new leader.

Change is always unsettling in an academic institution, where faculty members often serve far longer than presidents. But not only was Conway a woman; she was a feminist and quite clearly committed to women's education. In deciding to come to Smith, Conway describes the factors that led her to consider returning to the United States: "I was a feminist and that was a universal cause, to be served wherever the environment offered the greatest opportunity for leadership. It was a heady time in the feminist movement, but I knew feminism was a cyclical phenomenon, so one could have the greatest impact by strengthening institutions that kept it alive in all environments, and I knew they were in the United States."[3]

The primary question before her as she understood it from her initial interviews with the search committee was, "How could Smith's pioneering history and mission be restated, redefined, and enlarged to make it the outstanding leader in women's education for the next quarter century?"[4]

Resolution

The campus soon learned that Conway had a number of initiatives in mind. She was eager to establish a research program on women's lives, she wished to see the college's athletic program overhauled and expanded, and she wanted to see the college on a secure financial basis. Closest to her heart was a desire to address the educational needs of women who had experienced an interruption in their education.

But to enact any aspects of her program meant serious attention to the challenges facing the college. Recent decisions by several of the Ivies to admit women meant that Smith would face admissions competition from the newly co-ed elite institutions. The new leader was sanguine about this challenge: "It didn't matter in the least that all the Ivies were going co-educational. I knew there were enough bright women needing an education to go around."[5]

Despite her optimism about meeting the challenges from *off* campus, the new president faced more daunting issues *on* campus surrounding governance rules. In 1975, the college instituted new written rules concerning the processes governing personnel reviews for tenure and promotion. The faculty and trustees were still grappling with the development of written policies on these weighty matters.[6] Consequently, faculty attention was geared toward concerns about employment and academic freedom. Faculty meetings were consumed with debates over the wording of the new policies and the powers of the new grievance committee that were established as part of the procedural changes. At the same time, the trustees asked the new president to establish a better balance between tenured and untenured faculty. This exacerbated the challenges of writing a code for faculty review that was acceptable to all parties. To add to the complexity of the issues facing the new president, a budget overrun from the previous year left her with a looming deficit in the financial aid budget.

Conway's battles were legion in the first years of her administration. They included battles over feminist scholarship and how it might best be pursued and how to reform athletics and physical education to make the programs more responsive to the emerging requirements of Title IX. In both instances, Conway found a way to outmaneuver the opposition. With respect to a feminist research center, she skirted faculty opposition by funding the effort through a foundation grant. With regard to reforming athletics, she made a strategic appointment of a well-regarded male professor from the most conservative clique of the faculty. A firm believer in the importance of athletic competition for women, he happily championed the expansion of the athletic program, and it encountered very little faculty opposition.

Early in her presidency, Conway surveyed the Smith landscape, envisioned it as a battlefield, and launched her campaign for change in several directions. At its core, she recognized that the principal challenge before the college was financial and that this needed to be addressed immediately. She set about instructing herself in the financial situation and found a lifelong and trusted partner in the college treasurer, Robert Ellis. Ellis was delighted to have the new president's attention and explained the limits of the current financial model. He shared Conway's vision and goals for the college. He was an excellent tutor on the looming budgetary issues, and over her tenure and beyond, he proved to be a trusted source of friendship and financial guidance.[7]

Conway next asked for the help of key trustees in introducing her to the corporate financial world, where she would seek new avenues of support for the college. Not having gone to school with an old-boys network of well-connected friends who had gone on to have Wall Street careers, Conway needed to construct her own network to help navigate the financial world. She found that group among members of the Smith board of trustees who became her willing allies, making phone calls that opened doors to friends and colleagues. Once the introductions were made and Conway had a chance to discuss her plans, the financial support followed. In addition, this group of financially savvy supporters provided Conway with the guidance she needed to make the most of the world of corporate finance and private philanthropy.

On campus, she set about improving communications and fundraising. Conway saw the need to update methods and adopt a more aggressive approach to finding the resources to develop the educational projects that would put the college at the forefront of liberal arts colleges. This meant utilizing and energizing the superb network of Smith alumnae who were loyal to the college and accustomed to seeing Smith as a favored recipient of their charitable donations. Conway spent her first years tirelessly visiting alumnae groups across the United States. When the new campaign (Response to the Future) was launched in 1977, she attended every campaign opening across the country. The campaign easily exceeded its $40 million goal in just three and a half years (at the time, a record for liberal arts colleges). But Conway was not content with limiting fundraising to this traditional source. She wanted Smith to develop a base in the corporate and foundation worlds, and consequently, she accepted invitations to a number of corporate boards to build a network of corporate support and enhance her understanding of what Smith should offer its students to allow them access to leadership in the corporate world.

At the same time as she launched her fundraising campaign, and with the enormous energy of a leader in her prime, Conway launched the Ada Comstock Scholars Program that was closest to her heart.[8] She pursued the development of a program to provide wider access to a Smith education for older women and women who had had their education interrupted but wished to complete it. In the course of establishing the Ada Comstock program, she also launched a revolutionary program that would provide highly qualified women on welfare—that is, those who received Aid to Families with Dependent Children (AFDC) funds—with access to a Smith education. The story of both initiatives is at the heart of this study in women's leadership in higher education.

Just as 1975 was a different world for women's leadership in higher education, so too was the world of continuing education. Programs existed, but what existed in universities was often a combination of technical and vocational offerings. There were few such programs at the nation's leading liberal arts colleges. There, the undergraduate model was a young person aged eighteen to twenty-two enrolled in a four-year course of study, taking four or five courses each semester. For older women who wished to complete a bachelor's degree, access to a rigorous curriculum on the same terms as traditional undergraduates was simply not available. Furthermore, thinking about the needs of women returning to college, often with children and family responsibilities, was completely innovative. Nevertheless, it was exactly this situation that Conway would make one of the central goals of her tenure at Smith:

> I'd been working on the establishment of a part-time college at the University of Toronto, devoted to meeting the educational needs of returning students. A very high percentage were women, and the dropout rate for them was the highest in the entire educational system. . . . What could be achieved if an elite college for women began to take older women seriously, to give them financial aid and all the services necessary to maximize their talents? What about bright mothers trapped on welfare, whose lives could be transformed by education? Underneath all these questions was my sadness that my super intelligent mother had never had the chance for an education she'd have used so well. . . . She was the reason I'd never stopped trying to expand women's opportunities and why I wanted to make schools and colleges treat older women with genuine respect for their intellect and curiosity.[9]

The Ada Comstock program proved to be the ideal vehicle for pursuing Conway's goal. Of course, as with any innovation, there were obstacles and objections. Some members of the board of trustees worried that the development of the program would have deleterious effects on Smith's reputation: Would the program admit those who had failed by dropping out during their undergraduate careers? Would standards be lowered by the presence of older women, distracted perhaps by the demands of marriage or children? Would admissions standards be lowered? Would older students dominate classroom conversations or intimidate younger students?

Conway remained undaunted by such questions. She recognized the legitimacy of the concerns and those who expressed them. She needed allies and supporters among her trustees, so she addressed their concerns directly. She quelled many of the financial fears by agreeing that none of the scholarship aid currently designated for the traditional undergraduates would be diverted to the new program for returning older students. Financial aid would need to be provided, and often more aid would be needed because of the very different circumstances and responsibilities of older women. But the new president reached an understanding with the trustees that additional funds would be raised for the Ada program. And Conway was confident that she could raise the money. Moreover, she received significant support from the male members of the Smith board who worked in the corporate world and often had talented employees whose careers they wished to promote and whom they knew would benefit by a program such as the Ada Comstock Scholars. Conway found the enthusiastic support of this group of men, her financial brain trust, invaluable as she set about locating support for the fledgling program.

Despite the obstacles she faced, several factors weighed heavily in her favor as she launched the initiative. First, Smith's faculty had previously approved a version of the program in the spring of 1975, prior to Conway's arrival on campus. In addition, this endeavor had been proposed initially by members of the faculty, approved by the curriculum committee, and voted into existence by the trustees. Thus it did not become hostage to the ongoing battles over tenure and promotion or the concerns about feminist scholarship currently occupying faculty energies. In a second strategic move, Conway quickly identified the recently appointed assistant director, Eleanor Rothman, as the right person to lead the fledgling program.

Finally, the program had acquired a propitious name, the Ada Comstock Scholars Program. Thus there could be no confusion of this academic endeavor with the stigmatized continuing education. The women who came to Smith were identified as scholars, and this immediately gave a group identity and a sense of common purpose to the new, nontraditional "Smithies."

As soon as Conway arrived on campus in the summer of 1975, she turned her attention to the program. Eleanor Rothman's appointment as the assistant director of the program also began in July 1975, and Conway initiated regular meetings with her. Rothman was married to a senior member of the Smith government department and, consequently, was well acquainted with both the faculty and administration. She knew how the college worked and where to go to address the myriad problems that inevitably arise in any fledgling endeavor. The initial group of Adas (Ada scholars) consisted of thirty-five students, and the problems attendant upon a decidedly different group of students were immediately apparent. Besides tuition scholarships, the program had to resolve housing, scheduling, meals, childcare, integration with traditional students, and resting and study space for the scholars. Rothman had the energy, intelligence, and commitment to address them all. A graduate of Radcliffe, Rothman had just finished a successful teaching career in the chemistry department at a local private school. A working mother herself, she was sympathetic to the challenges facing the Adas and able to provide advice and guidance from that shared experience. In confirming Rothman's appointment, Conway said she was looking for a person with a passion for the program. She found that in Eleanor Rothman, and the two worked in close collaboration as they took on the myriad challenges of the program.[10]

First was the matter of housing. Dorm living was a possibility for some of the single Adas but not for most. Would women in their thirties and forties find life in proximity to eighteen- to twenty-year-olds manageable? Married Adas and those with children needed their own apartments, and Northampton had a limited supply of one- and two-bedroom apartments. Smith had a stock of apartments and houses intended for the use of new faculty members relocating to the region. Could the Adas claim some of those? Could current Smith student dormitories be repurposed for the needs of women with children?

The Adas themselves were creative in their efforts to solve housing problems. Because Smith had an unusual class schedule— Monday through Wednesday for some classes and Wednesday through Friday for others—it was possible for Adas to plan their class schedules in such a way as to meet three days a week and share an apartment with another Ada with classes at the opposite end of the week. This took some planning and flexibility, but it also helped alleviate the housing problem.

Adas who commuted from a distance presented another challenge. Where would these students find a congenial space for resting between classes? What would they do with their children while they spent the required hours in the library (in the days before the internet and computer access)? How would this new group of older students socialize and mix with traditional undergraduates outside the classroom? Both Rothman and Conway understood the importance of the new social networks and mutual support systems the Adas needed to establish, and they also anticipated the mutually beneficial impact of intergenerational contact on students and the college.

Dining was another issue. At the time the program was founded in the mid-1970s, Smith dining was provided in the student houses. Social life in the student houses was (and is) an important part of the undergraduate experience, and dining together was part of that experience. Would Adas be welcome in the houses, and how could financial arrangements be organized to make dining in student houses possible? Would Adas be welcome at Friday afternoon teas, a hallowed Smith house tradition? A house affiliation program quickly emerged, and Conway and Rothman made sure that every Ada who wished to have a house affiliation did. Some of the Adas were assigned housing in the faculty suites, and Adas sometimes assumed the role of informal counselors—though without holding a formal position or receiving compensation.

Conway was apprised of every concern that emerged with the new program, and there is ample evidence from the president's correspondence that no need was too small for the president's attention. Rothman knew she had the president's support and felt confident that Conway would do her utmost to address the Adas' concerns. In summing up Conway's influence on the program, Rothman said, "The reason that the Ada Comstock program flourished (and still exists) is that, in the critical early years, it had unwavering support from the highest levels of the administration."[11]

The need for an Ada lounge, a social space designated for this new group, was a high priority. A temporary lounge was located in the library, and soon thereafter a more adequate and adaptable space was founded in a building on the edge of campus where limited student parking was also available. The president's correspondence indicates that she was peppered with requests for renovated refrigerators, improved telephone service, and mail delivery. The president took all such requests seriously and arranged to meet with the Adas at the monthly luncheons as often as her schedule permitted.

She frequently rearranged her schedule to meet with the Adas, and she was a willing participant in the Adas' annual Rally Day skits. Throughout her tenure, Conway told me, she was an accessible and enthusiastic supporter of the Adas, aware of their courage and appreciative of the challenges they faced. They registered in droves for the president's seminar on the history of women reformers and treasured the weekly sessions in the president's living room.

A key factor in the success of the program was that it enjoyed wide popularity among the faculty. The presence of the Adas in Smith classrooms was a welcome addition for most faculty members. The seriousness with which the Adas undertook their studies meant that they easily acquired faculty mentors and sponsors. Many Adas established strong ties to the faculty, and this also translated into continuing support for the college and the program once the Adas became Smith alums.

Academic concerns also had to be addressed. The program was established with a clear expectation that, initially, Adas would not be required to carry full loads of courses. This recognized that most of these women had family responsibilities (a husband, partner, or children) and that many were still holding down a job or commuting to campus (sometimes from significant distances). Thus their tuition charges could be prorated by the number of courses they undertook. This required the controller and financial aid offices to recognize that a uniform bill for tuition, room, and board would not be appropriate for the Adas. Initially, there was resistance to the need for flexibility, but the president's intervention and the appointment of a new controller solved this issue. Nevertheless, the requirement that the scholarship aid for traditional undergraduates could not be used to support the Adas meant that identifying new sources of financial aid was a pressing and immediate need if the program was to survive and prosper.

Fortunately, Conway was a masterful fundraiser, and the launching of a new campaign for Smith in 1977, Response to the Future, gave her the opportunity to target the entire alumnae body for raising funds for financial aid for the Ada Comstock scholars. She ensured that the program was included in the goals of the campaign and reviewed, with care, every piece of material prepared to make the case for the program. She wanted to ensure that all materials for the campaign reflected her belief that there was nothing exceptional, odd, or strange about an older woman seeking to continue her education. She wanted older women's educational aspirations treated as normal and Smith known as a college that took all women's minds seriously regardless of age.

Her sense of the program's mission is reflected in the welcome she wrote for the *Handbook for Ada Comstock Scholars* in July 1978. In particular, she had great insight into the emotional challenges many of the Adas faced as they entered Smith. Would they be able to measure up? Had they taken on more than they could manage at a stage of life when they bore wider responsibilities for others than does the traditional undergraduate? Responding to those fears, she wrote, "Growth is not without its hazards and it is often painful for mature women to discard earlier patterns of acceptance of reduced expectations and learn to push themselves to the limits of achievement. The conflicts which come from this drive to develop one's full intellectual capacity as an adult with responsibilities and ties to others can only be resolved and coped with when shared. This is why we believe that Smith, as a community dedicated to women's education, has much to offer through the Ada Comstock Scholars Program."[12]

From the outset, Conway's vision for the program was wider than Smith. She saw opening educational opportunities for older women—or women who had had their college careers interrupted—as an item for the national education agenda. Within the first year, she and Rothman determined that this was a propitious moment for Smith to invite other colleges with similar programs or interest in establishing such programs to a joint meeting to share the lessons learned. Smith teamed with Wesleyan University in Middletown, Connecticut, to sponsor a daylong meeting at Smith in the fall of 1976. The Conference on Older Undergraduate Women took place on the Smith campus and received significant support from Alison Bernstein, who was then with the Ford Foundation and deeply concerned with the expansion of educational opportunities for minority women. Discussions at the meeting dealt with curricular problems, the similarities and differences found between traditional-age students and older students, and issues of counseling and guidance. Finding adequate financial support for older students was a critical concern for all institutions.

The Ford Foundation had sponsored a preliminary report that served as the background for the meeting. That report noted the failure of programs of continuing education to address the needs of minority women and women with limited resources, especially single women with children. Conway's talk at the conference, titled "Impact of Education for Older Undergraduates on the Institution," spoke of the Adas' effect on the curriculum, the residential community, extracurricular activities, women's life stages, and the trade-offs involved in multiple commitments, career counseling, the importance of female sociability, and the financial effect of such programs on college budgets. Throughout the development of the Ada Comstock program, Conway insisted on the reciprocal benefits of intergenerational contact among women and the positive benefits of the Ada population on the college community.[13]

With respect to the financial issues, Conway was quite explicit in 1976 that as yet, Smith did not have a clear idea of the overhead costs of the program. Nor was there a clear path to financing the Ada scholars, apart from raising funds for scholarships. The costs of recruiting nationally were as yet unknown, as were estimates of the costs of appropriate housing and social space.

Shortly after the Conference on Older Undergraduate Women meeting, the idea of a program for women receiving public assistance began to emerge as a result of a contact arranged by a member of the Smith faculty with a representative of the Charles Stewart Mott Foundation. A meeting was arranged between the program officer of the Mott Foundation and Conway, and from their conversations, the possibility of an experimental program emerged. The program supported by Mott would be for women on welfare who had the potential to complete a college degree and thereby change their economic circumstances and those of their families. In January 1977, Conway traveled to the headquarters of the Mott Foundation in Detroit to meet with foundation officers and discuss what might be possible. The Mott Foundation made it clear in the meeting and in subsequent communications that it was interested in addressing the issue of rural poverty in New England. Similarly, the foundation was interested in how further education might make possible new careers and new employment opportunities. It also insisted on a commitment from Smith that the college would attempt to raise an endowment for the Mott program and make support for it part of the regular operating budget.

The initial proposal was sent to the Mott Foundation in December 1977, and the funds for the first year of the program arrived in 1979, with the first group of Mott-supported women arriving in September 1979. The Mott program that eventually emerged called for admitting ten women on public assistance as students in the Ada Comstock Scholars program each year over the course of four years. It was meant as a pilot program to demonstrate the importance of providing women on welfare with educational opportunities that would allow them to break out of the welfare system. Because of its unique character, a great deal of learning occurred in the first years of the grant.

All the women on the Mott grant were receiving AFDC funds as well as other types of public assistance, such as that from the Work Incentive Program as well as food stamps (later known as SNAP). A primary concern in the first years was how to deliver financial assistance to the Adas without jeopardizing the public assistance they were receiving. Concurrent with the Mott program at Smith was an ongoing national discussion about reducing welfare spending and requiring recipients of welfare to work as opposed to study. How then to justify a program that appeared to some to be a luxury and very much against mainstream thought on welfare and work?

The argument that women needed a college education in order to find jobs that would keep their families from depending on welfare was not always persuasive with bureaucrats in the welfare office. The Adas with Mott scholarships feared that losing their AFDC funds would mean that they would no longer be able to continue their studies. The financial aid office quickly learned that direct payments to the Adas might risk losses to their public assistance. Hence the office developed a system of voucher or vendor payments to assist the Adas with rent and other nontuition expenses. Navigating the welfare system became a new challenge for Rothman and

Ann Keppler, the director of financial aid, but their willingness to take this on became a crucial aspect of the Mott program's success.[14]

Conway was well aware of the policy implications of the Mott program and eager to catalog its impact. The public climate regarding welfare had shifted with the advent of the Reagan administration in 1980, and there were increased demands to limit public subsidies and tie payments to a work requirement. As the success of the Mott scholars became evident, Conway decided that scholarly analysis of the outcomes of the Mott program might contribute to the public debate and increase appreciation for the impact of women's expanded access to higher education. To that end, she supported several studies of the program as well as a major conference in the spring of 1985 on women, welfare, and higher education.[15]

In her report of 1978–1979, Conway wrote, "The 1978–79 year also saw the number of Ada Comstock scholars grow to more than 100. . . . The governing idea behind the program has been the belief that a college for women has a responsibility to make a first-class undergraduate education available to qualified women and to do so in ways that recognize that economic and social barriers have prevented many talented women from seeking higher education at the traditional age."[16]

Conway goes on to emphasize the impact of the Adas on Smith, noting first that among these women, the drive for learning was equaled only by the determination to carry out family responsibilities while studying. The president noted that the experience of the Adas provided important insight into the lives of adult women in contemporary America and that traditional patterns of financial aid would not be sufficient to meet the needs of this group. The grants from the Mott Foundation would allow the college to experiment with new approaches to aiding this group of students that might well have implications for national programs to address the needs of women with families.

By 1981, when Smith had 184 Ada Comstock scholars enrolled, including twenty Mott scholars, Conway would write in her president's report what the college had discovered: "There was indeed a broad constituency of older women who could benefit from a Smith education, and whose families, too, in many instances, might find their circumstances transformed by the opportunities opened by their mother's access to Smith's educational facilities and faculty."[17]

The academic results of the Mott program were evident by 1984. As Conway detailed to me, of the twenty-four Mott-supported scholars who had graduated by 1984, eight had graduated cum laude and one magna cum laude, and six had been elected to Phi Beta Kappa. At least seven had gone on to pursue graduate degrees in law, theater, anthropology, education, comparative literature, and biological sciences.

By the time Conway left office in June 1985, the Adas were part of the permanent landscape of the student population at Smith. Over $1 million in foundation and corporate grants had been received for the program, and from 1984 on, all Adas with demonstrated need received aid from the college. Over twenty Adas had graduated and become a part of the alumnae body. Among these "nontraditional" students, winning an election to Phi Beta Kappa was not unusual, nor was appearing on the dean's list. Of the original forty Mott scholars, thirty-eight had graduated.[18] Adas had gone on to law school and graduate programs in a range of fields and had found employment in jobs that utilized their education. In 1985, as Conway retired from the presidency, she received tributes from all sectors of the college, and upon receiving a fond farewell from the 1985 Adas, she wrote,

> Nothing I have done at Smith has given me greater pleasure than the establishment of the Ada Comstock Scholars program and the commitment of funds to offer Adas financial aid. Each one of you individually and all of you collectively have given me great pride because of your achievements and your love of learning.
>
> It's wonderful to leave knowing that the program is very solidly established and will move on from strength to strength. You all made that happen by your academic achievements. It has been a privilege to be part of the process of seeing your talents developed and released.[19]

At the critical junctures of leadership, Conway had moved ahead to support the program with vigor and a careful strategy. She identified strong energetic leadership for the program and supported her appointee. She was fortunate to have strong faculty support for the program, which was an essential component in the program's success. She found broad-based funding for the program and addressed the legitimate concerns of those who doubted the viability and wisdom of the endeavor. And she found a way to make the lessons learned more broadly shared so that additional women might benefit from access to comparable educational opportunities. Her decision to seek a scholarly assessment of the program meant that the public policy implications of the program as well as the lessons learned were widely available and the program could be replicated.[20]

Notes

1   The announcement appeared on the front page of the *New York Times* and noted that Smith was the last of the Seven Sisters to appoint a woman president.

2   This personal history is retold in rich detail in Conway's *New York Times* best sellers *The Road from Coorain* (New York: Alfred A. Knopf, 1989) and *True North* (New York: Alfred A. Knopf, 1994).

3   Jill Ker Conway, *A Woman's Education* (New York: Alfred A. Knopf, 2001), 16.

4   Ibid., 14.

5   Ibid., 15.

6   The new written procedures were in response to legal challenges from three faculty members denied tenure in the early 1970s. This was a highly contentious matter that led to several lawsuits. This recent history added to tensions surrounding the development of the new rules.

7   Jill Ker Conway, in discussions with the author, October 2015, November 2015, and December 2015. All direct quotes and statements are taken from these interviews unless otherwise noted.

8   Ada Comstock was a Smith graduate of the class of 1897. She returned to Smith as dean in 1910 and served the college until she became president of Radcliffe in 1923.

9   Conway, *Woman's Education*, 22.

10   Conway, reflecting on this key appointment, noted that when you find the right person for a position, you need to back her up and get out of the way. Ellie Rothman served as director of the Ada Comstock Program until 1998. See Conway, *Road from Coorain*.

11   Eleanor Rothman, in discussion with the author, February 23, 2018. I would like to thank Ellie for her thoughtful comments on an earlier draft of this essay.

12   Jill Ker Conway, *Handbook for Ada Comstock Scholars* (Northampton, Mass.: Smith College, 1978).

13   A report on the Conference on Older Women Students is found in the Smith
     College Archives in the collection of Conway's presidential papers on the Ada
     Comstock Program.

14   Jill Ker Conway, interview by Eleanor Rothman, Northampton, Mass., October
     2016.

15   See the excellent volume containing the papers from the conference, Martha A.
     Ackelsberg, Randall Bartlett, and Robert Buchele, eds., *Women, Welfare
     and Higher Education: Toward Comprehensive Policies* (Northampton, Mass.:
     Smith College, 1988).

16   Jill Ker Conway, *Report of the President, 1978–79* (Northampton, Mass.: Smith
     College, 1979).

17   Jill Ker Conway, *Report of the President, 1980–81* (Northampton, Mass.:
     Smith College, 1980), 9–10.

18   Of the two who did not graduate, one withdrew from the program and one
     died in a car accident.

19   Jill Ker Conway, letter to Beverly Fonner, Ada Comstock Scholars Program
     class of 1985, May 29, 1985, Smith College Archives, Jill Conway presidential
     papers on the Ada Comstock Scholars Program. I would like to express thanks
     to Nanci Young of the Smith College Archives and the librarians of the Sophia
     Smith Collection for their assistance in the research for this essay.

20   At the end of her presidency, Conway resisted every attempt by the Smith
     trustees to name a building after her. She only relented years later when, under
     the presidency of Carol Christ, the college named a new apartment complex
     built explicitly for Ada Comstock students with children, the Conway House.
     Jill Conway attended the opening and expressed her delight at this addition to
     the college landscape.

Intellectual Inquiry and Social Activism

Sister President Johnnetta Betsch Cole

Marilyn R. Schuster

> If we do nothing to improve our world, then we cannot call ourselves educated women. How can we call ourselves either educated or leaders if we turn away from the reality that a third of black America lives in poverty? We must build sturdy black bridges into the very communities from which we have come and into those which surround us.
>
> —Johnnetta Betsch Cole, inaugural address as president of Spelman College, November 6, 1987

Background

In 1976, Don Stewart, a distinguished African American academic educated at Grinnell College, Yale, and Harvard universities, was chosen by the Spelman board of trustees to become the college's sixth president. Students demonstrated outside the trustees' meeting, effectively locking them in; outraged, they demanded that the board appoint instead an African American woman to lead the college.[1] The trustees held firm. When Johnnetta Betsch Cole was chosen eleven years later, students were jubilant to have a "sister" president at last. Don Stewart, who supported Cole, would introduce himself amiably by saying, "I'm Don Stewart, the last male president of Spelman College for women."

Expectations were very high when Johnnetta Betsch Cole assumed the presidency of Spelman College. Alumnae, students, trustees, and friends expected Cole to establish Spelman as the top historically black college in the country, to create a national profile for the women's college, to increase applications, and to grow the campus and the endowment. An unspoken assumption was that the first sister president would exemplify the qualities of leadership the college sought to inspire in its students. In an interview for the New York Times just after her appointment, Cole mused that the trustees had not made a "safe choice, since I am a divorced woman associated with women's studies and Afro-American studies who has raised disturbing questions within mainstream anthropology."[2] Safe choices, however, don't always move institutions forward in difficult times. Three factors especially would shape her leadership: a campus culture unlike the institutions she had known, the need to raise funds in the wake of the 1987 crash of global markets, and a changing landscape in higher education that tested the viability of women's colleges and historically black colleges and universities. A brief look at the history of the college and at her personal story helps one understand why Johnnetta Cole, though not a safe choice for Spelman in 1987, was the right choice.

Founded in 1881, Spelman had grown in its first 106 years from a small school for African American girls in a church basement to a respected liberal arts college for women situated on a well-groomed campus and sustained by an endowment of $41 million. The Atlanta Baptist Female Seminary for African American women and girls was founded by two white women from New England, Sophia B. Packard and Harriet E. Giles, who were able to open the seminary with gifts from religious organizations and northern philanthropists. Three years later, Packard and Giles received a significant gift from John D. Rockefeller, and the school was renamed Spelman Seminary to honor his wife, Laura Spelman, and her family, who had been abolitionists. Packard and then Giles led the seminary until Giles's death in 1909.

In the early years, the seminary served the younger grades and high school students; the pupils learned practical skills as well as academic subjects. In 1909, another white woman from New England, Lucy Tapley, became president. During her seventeen years as Spelman's leader, the school shifted from elementary and secondary education to college-level courses as other opportunities for young African American girls in Georgia increased. In 1927, Florence Read, a Mount Holyoke College alumna who had worked at the Rockefeller Foundation, was named president. During her twenty-six years as president, Spelman Seminary became Spelman College and developed a liberal arts curriculum. In 1929, Spelman joined with other area black institutions to establish the Atlanta University Center Consortium, which included Morris Brown, Clark Atlanta University, Spelman College, Morehouse College, and eventually, the Morehouse School of Medicine. Read was the first president to establish an endowment when she took office that grew to $3 million during her term.

In 1953, Spelman appointed the first African American and first male president, Albert E. Manley. Under his leadership, Spelman became fully accredited by the Southern Association of Colleges and Secondary Schools. Although students had objected to Don Stewart's appointment in 1976, the college thrived under his leadership, and in 1981, Spelman became the first historically black college to establish a research and resource center for women.

Johnnetta Betsch Cole speaks with the rich, precise cadence of a seasoned orator, her voice resonating with echoes of her southern childhood sharpened by years of civil rights and feminist activism. Born in Jacksonville, Florida, in 1936, Johnnetta Betsch grew up in the Jim Crow South, the wretched days of sanctioned racism—legal segregation, as she has said. But at home, she enjoyed the privileges of a warm, well-educated, economically comfortable family. In 1901, her great-grandfather Abraham Lincoln Lewis established the Afro-American Life Insurance Company with a group of his peers. Their goal was to provide more financial security to African Americans at a time "when no white insurance company would touch a black body."[3] He and his cofounders thought that passing the plate every

Sunday was an inefficient way to look after the community. At one point, the company had offices in Georgia, Florida, Alabama, and Texas. A. L. Lewis became Jacksonville's first black millionaire and used his wealth for philanthropic purposes, including support for black colleges. He died when Johnnetta was eleven, but his voice resonates in her memory even today: "My great-grandfather A. L. Lewis repeatedly quoted Micah to me; and then he would ask, 'What doth the Lord expect of thee today?' And every Sunday in Sunday school where he was the superintendent, 'What will you do for the race?'"[4] Johnnetta was taught from a very early age that education and service were twin expectations for a meaningful life.

Both of Cole's parents, educated at black colleges, eventually worked for the family insurance company. Her mother had also served as an English teacher and registrar at Edward Waters College, the oldest black college in Jacksonville. Segregation barred the young Johnnetta Betsch from art museums and concerts, but her mother filled their house with reproductions of art and recordings of classical music. Teachers and librarians made a lasting impression throughout her education. When her first-grade teacher asked the students to give their names on the first day of school, Cole recalls, "I remember mumbling my name as best I could; and I remember Mrs. Bunny Vance standing in front of me and with the full force of her voice saying, 'Stand up, look me straight in the eye and never again as long as you live mumble who you are.'"[5]

School was supplemented by frequent trips to the library. Cole states, "I think of Olga Bradham, the librarian in the A. L. Lewis Colored Branch of the Jacksonville Public Library. I don't think that it would be possible to count the number of African American women and men of my age who were influenced by Olga Bradham, who simply loved books, who believed that every black kid had the possibility of just surrounding themselves with the magic of learning."[6] In the South that Johnnetta Betsch knew, when African Americans were excluded from white schools, museums, libraries, and insurance companies, they created their own institutions to develop the minds and self-confidence of the young.

When Fisk University instituted an early admissions program, Cole's parents encouraged her to take the entry exam; she passed it easily and skipped the twelfth grade to enter Fisk at the age of fifteen. Although she only stayed for a year, she says that Fisk opened up for her "the world of the intellectual." She remembers that "simply being in the presence of a black intellectual like Harlem Renaissance poet Arna Bontemps, who was the librarian at Fisk and a man of letters," had a profound influence on her.[7]

Her father died when Cole was at Fisk; seeking solace, she transferred to Oberlin College, where her older sister was a student. Having lived in black Christian communities her whole life, Oberlin was somewhat of a culture shock for the young student. She was struck by the diversity of backgrounds she encountered there and, as at Fisk, by the wealth of resources that helped her as she mourned the loss of her father. She found comfort in the Allen Memorial Art Museum, "a place of such healing that [she] had a personal, visceral understanding of the healing power of art."[8]

When she entered college, Cole's ambition was to become a pediatrician, a profession her parents applauded. It was at Oberlin that she discovered anthropology through a charismatic teacher, George Eaton Simpson, whom she describes as "a very tall, lanky white sociologist who, in his heart, and really much of his training, was an anthropologist, who, in one class, moved me from pediatrics to anthropology."[9] He had lived and studied in black communities and institutions, and he taught about the retention of African culture in the New World. Cole received her BA in 1957. She then went on to receive an MA (1959) and a PhD (1967) in anthropology from Northwestern. In graduate school, she met Robert Cole, a white graduate student in economics who shared her interest in Africa; they married in 1960 before doing fieldwork for a year in Liberia. Johnnetta gave birth to the first of their three sons during that year.

When they returned, they took teaching positions at Washington State University. She cofounded one of the first black studies programs in the country and was named Outstanding Teacher of the Year in 1965. In 1970, the Coles left Washington to join the faculty at the University of Massachusetts at Amherst.

Just as Cole was committed early on to the development of black studies, she became active in women's studies at the University of

Massachusetts. As she taught the introductory course in women's studies at Massachusetts, she asked, "Where are the black women?" and worked for a more inclusive curriculum. She also learned the importance of considering sexual identities in the classroom and in the curriculum. Johnnetta became the associate provost for undergraduate education before leaving Massachusetts in 1983 to join the faculty at Hunter College in New York, where she also directed the Latin American and Caribbean studies program. A year earlier, the Coles had divorced.

At Hunter, one of Cole's most powerful mentors was her colleague Audre Lorde, poet laureate of New York, who often introduced herself as "Audre Lorde, a black, woman, lesbian, professor, mother, poet, warrior." She impressed on Cole the inseparability of multiple identities, a theoretical concept later articulated as "intersectionality" by Kimberlé Crenshaw.[10] As Cole asked hard questions of mainstream anthropology and participated in black studies and women's studies, she did the hard inner work, as she calls it, to identify blind spots and unacknowledged bias in her own thinking as she broadened the base of her scholarship and teaching. Intense self-scrutiny linked to intellectual growth; a deep connection between self and community, between personal and social commitments, are woven into the fabric of her story.

Donna Shalala, president of Hunter, recommended Cole to Marian Edelman, the chair of the Spelman College board of trustees, who was chairing a presidential search committee for a successor to Donald Stewart in 1986. At first, Cole resisted, saying that her administrative experience was limited. But she relented and became a candidate. Three factors would shape Cole's presidency at Spelman: campus culture, financial resources, and the changing landscape of American higher education.

Resolution

Cole embraced the role of sister president, and the campus welcomed her warmly, especially the students. At the same time, she reflects, "Some very peculiar things happened as a result of

Spelman's history and mine coming into the same place."[11] When asked by Julian Bond what had surprised her when she arrived in Atlanta, Cole responded that the faculty seemed to be quietly stone-walling her. She would advance ideas and they wouldn't object; they would just avoid responding or engaging with what she proposed.

Ever the anthropologist, the new president wanted to under-stand the roots of the attitudes she encountered, to uncover the histories that might explain the campus culture and enable her to interact more effectively. Cole had left the South at the age of six-teen when she went to Oberlin. Most of her college years and all her professional experiences were in predominantly white, northern institutions—most recently in New York—where open argument, often emphatic, was the norm. The faculties she had belonged to were used to taking on the administration, jealous of their own power in making decisions. She recalled that at most historically black colleges, authority had been firmly lodged in the president's office. Decision-making was traditionally top-down, in part because often, decisions had to be quick in response to hostile social con-ditions. Faced with this dilemma, she reflects, "I had to reconnect with my southernness. I had not lived in the South since that one year at Fisk, 1953 to '54. And so, I really took some counsel there with myself, and I started reading about and thinking about 'What is the nature of being Southern?' And once I reconnected with a good deal of that, I'm not saying that it solved the problem, but it helped me to administer far better. Secondly, I really think that my own openness was useful. It made me accessible. It diffused some of the sense of 'Here comes the president.'"[12]

In reconnecting with her southernness, Cole realized that what appeared to be stonewalling was a deeply rooted avoidance of con-flict compounded by the lack of a history of shared governance. She resolved to strengthen shared governance—to involve fac-ulty, staff, and students in decision-making. She says, "My style of leadership is clearly centered [on] the concept of collaboration. Maybe it's because I'm chicken; I don't want to be the one to make all the decisions and take all the blame. Whatever the reason, I have seen repeatedly the value of collaboration over singularity in leader-ship. The very idea of shared governance is lodged in the concept of collaboration. It's built on the notion of teamwork; it calls for broad-scale participation. I just don't think that, ultimately, the best decisions are made in isolation by a single individual or a small group of individuals."

Colleagues elsewhere, especially administrators and trustees, were surprised that she wanted to give up power, to share it widely. But her conviction was that shared decision-making makes for a more vital, engaged campus. Difficult and time-consuming in the short run, shared governance is better for the institution in the long run. She was serious about including students and staff and being as transparent as possible with hard issues to keep the whole campus informed.

Another surprise when she arrived was the discovery that Spelman was not a feminist campus even though there were feminists on the faculty, including Beverly Guy-Sheftall, a Spelman alumna and tenured faculty member who had become the founding director of the Spelman Women's Research and Resource Center in 1981. Cole was surprised that there was not more widespread identification with feminist issues because the trustees hired her knowing that she was outspoken as a feminist. In one early episode, she encountered backlash when, in concert with feminist faculty members, she made a decision too quickly. At Sisters' Chapel early in her term, Cole announced the intention to establish an organization to support lesbian and bisexual students. "It did not go over well," she says in a marked understatement. She was surprised because it seemed a timely effort to her in 1987; one of her goals when she arrived was to create a more inclusive campus—to value religious and sexual diversity. But the campus wasn't ready. More than twenty years later, in 2011, the Women's Research and Resource Center sponsored a summit for historically black colleges and universities (HBCUs) to create dialogue about lesbian, gay, bisexual, and transgender issues on black college campuses. Six years later, Spelman was the first historically black college to develop a positive policy about admission for transgender students, and in 2017, Beverly Guy-Sheftall created the Dr. Levi Watkins Jr. Scholars Program as well as a companion lecture series at Spelman that explores contemporary issues of race, gender, and sexuality.[13]

On reflection, Cole noted that her experience at Spelman and later as president at Bennett College, also a historically black women's college in North Carolina, showed her that what appears to be social conservatism at these colleges goes hand in hand with activism for social change. While they may have a reputation as white-glove schools, steeped in traditions that required women to dress and behave as ladies even as they were also expected to become leaders in their communities and in the world, the reputation fails to take into account both the deep and the more recent history of black womanhood in the South.[14] The mission of the nineteenth-century Black Women's Club movement and of historically black colleges was to counter white supremacists' demeaning and over-sexualizing of black bodies by upholding high standards of decorum and dress and by preparing women for productive lives. Cole states,

> I think it's important to remember the history and herstory of these institutions. That good old African proverb—you've got to look back in order to go forward—or as the folks who reared me said, "You can't tell where you're going until you know where you've been." These were institutions that had come through incredibly awful times—with [the] KKK coming on the campuses, burning crosses—leading to a kind of conservatism that was in reaction to circumstances. The best example: Spelman and Bennett had a history of women wearing their pearls, carrying their pocketbooks, [putting] their little hats on to go downtown, and while one could say, "C'mon, put on a pair of blue jeans," it was like armor in the South at a given era that said to white men, "Don't you dare!" So that's why I think before we start so easily critiquing the norms and the mores of a campus like Spelman or Bennett, you have to say, What did they come through to be where they were?

Spelman and Bennett, like other historically black colleges, supported an activist agenda. At both Bennett and Spelman, students were among the first to plan and to implement sit-ins at local businesses during the early years of the civil rights movement. They participated in voter registration drives. They were supported by their presidents even when they went to jail for their civil disobedience.

During her presidency, Cole continued and extended the tradition of service to the community, a tradition she had learned by the example of her own family. Speaking about goals for women's colleges specifically and higher education more generally, she says that a fundamental goal is to help students figure out their role in changing the world for the better and how to realize it: "I have never seen social activism as separate from intellectual inquiry. Most folk will easily say you've got to have intellectual inquiry, maybe they'll say you've got to have some social activism—but I want to say that social activism needs to be informed by intellectual inquiry. I think we are best in our efforts for social justice when we have some sense of where and why and when it didn't exist."

To sustain excellence and engagement, a college needs a sound financial footing. Cole is the first to acknowledge that Don Stewart handed over a Spelman that was in good financial shape, with a dedicated faculty and staff and well-qualified students. Cole also recognizes the good work of all her predecessors, beginning with the white women from New England, whose vision and commitment to the education of African American girls and women made it all possible. Two white philanthropic families had provided significant funding historically: the Rockefellers and the Rosenwalds. Gifts from these two families "provided the seed corn on which Spelman would go on to build a significant endowment."[15] But recognizing the need to broaden the base of the endowment, Stewart was the first Spelman president to professionalize fundraising at the college; he led the first capital campaign in the college's history and raised $12 million during his term.

During the search process when a faculty member asked Cole about her fundraising experience, she candidly admitted that it was limited. She had successfully competed for grants to support her research but had not done the donor cultivation basic to presidential fundraising. Any lingering faculty misgivings about her lack of experience disappeared when, at her inauguration ceremony, Cole was able to announce that Bill and Camille Cosby, close friends since her tenure at the University of Massachusetts, were making a $20 million gift to Spelman. Sixty percent of the gift would be used to establish the Camille Olivia Hanks Cosby Academic Center; the remainder would be used to endow chairs in the fine arts, social sciences, and humanities. This was the largest gift ever received by a historically black college and the first large family gift from an African American family.[16]

Another major gift came as a welcome surprise early in her term. Stewart, during his capital campaign, had brokered an agreement with the DeWitt Wallace Foundation, funded by the publishers of *Reader's Digest*. The details of the agreement had been largely forgotten by the business officers by 1987. The agreement involved annual scholarship gifts from a $1 million endowed fund on the condition that the DeWitt Wallace Foundation would manage the fund for ten to fifteen years because they were unsure of the college's ability to manage the gift.[17] At the beginning of Cole's term, the foundation invited Cole and Danny Flanigan, Spelman's vice president for business and financial affairs and treasurer, to meet with officers of the organization at their headquarters in New York. The terms of the gift had been forgotten over the years, and Cole and Flanigan were unaware that the $1 million gift of *Reader's Digest* stocks had grown to $42 million. When they went to New York, they learned that the foundation now had confidence in the college's ability to manage the gift and was transferring the responsibility to them. They were grateful but concerned that such a large portion of the Spelman endowment would be concentrated in a single stock. The foundation agreed to their request to diversify over a one-year period. The decision turned out to be a wise one because shortly after they diversified, *Reader's Digest* stocks plummeted in value.

A few years into her presidency, Cole launched a new capital campaign that raised $115 million. Of that total, $113.8 million went to the endowment, growing it from $41 million to $141 million at the end of the campaign. Spelman now had the largest endowment for a historically black college or university. The successful campaign and the growth of the endowment and programs that Spelman established during Cole's presidency brought national attention. The college's rankings increased appreciably in *U.S. News & World Report*, the Association of Medical Colleges, and *Money Guide* magazine's "Best College Buys Now." In 1995, Spelman was among the first six institutions (and the only college) to receive recognition by the

National Science Foundation and National Aeronautics and Space Administration Model Institutions for Excellence program, an initiative established to increase the number of underrepresented minorities in science, technology, engineering, and mathematics.

The association with the Cosby family also increased positive visibility for Spelman during Cole's presidency. The shots of the campus buildings and entrance to the fictional Hillman College, the site of Bill Cosby's popular television series *A Different World* (1987–1993), were of Spelman. The national visibility and the development of new academic programs were especially important because the landscape of higher education was changing in a way that threatened women's colleges and HBCUs.

By 1987, most predominantly white men's colleges had become coeducational, and many women's colleges had merged with men's universities or had been unable to sustain their historic mission. Many, from Vassar in 1967 to Goucher in 1986, had become coeducational; others closed their doors, unable to compete for students. By 1987, more than twenty-five HBCUs had failed. By the late 1980s, most white-dominated colleges and universities had aggressively reached out to students of color in an attempt to increase diversity on their campuses. Bright young African American women were actively recruited by the most prestigious colleges and universities in the country. Similarly, faculty of color were sought to diversify faculties that were almost exclusively white. Many people assumed that by 1987, niche institutions like women's colleges and HBCUs were no longer necessary. These small and vulnerable colleges were seen by outsiders as vestiges of sexism, exposed by the women's movement in the 1970s, and of sanctioned segregation, illegal since 1964. Richly resourced male- and white-dominated institutions assumed that they offered a superior education to women's and black colleges and universities.

Spelman was caught in the crosshairs of both trends. Cole's experience as a faculty member and administrator in predominantly white institutions had taught her, however, that racist assumptions, explicit and unconscious, did not disappear with segregation. She notes that even the best predominantly white coeducational institutions are "haunted by racism and sexism."[18] In contrast, at Spelman, there was no assumption that "black folks don't like math and women cannot do science. There is no assumption that women are just not as bright as men and will never understand economics as easily as men do. On the contrary, the assumption is that Spelman women will excel in all of their studies."[19]

Black women students at Spelman saw themselves reflected in the faculty and staff and as student leaders and successful athletes. Cole knew from her own upbringing that even in the depths of Jim Crow racism, a nurturing black community provides positive models that build self-esteem. The need did not disappear when racist assumptions became less obvious. Spelman's best course, Cole believed, was to continue to do everything it could to strengthen the quality of the college. Toward the beginning of her term, Cole observed that Spelman had "tightened itself intellectually . . . one sees an improved general education curriculum, one sees a higher percentage of faculty with PhDs or with terminal degrees in their disciplines, and one sees the attraction of exciting projects and proposals all the way from computer literacy to gender balance in the curriculum. All of that is a part of creating the notion that here is not only an all-black institution, or 99 percent black, but a black institution of quality."[20]

In 1998–1999, thirty-seven percent of Spelman students majored in math, the sciences, computer science, and a dual-degree program in engineering, while the national average for African American students hovers at 10 percent.[21] The $25 million renovation and expansion of the science center, supported by the successful capital campaign, would enhance those numbers. Just as important, Cole points out, the faculty cares about teaching, and they have high expectations for Spelman students in all fields. The students can spend all their energy on their studies without having to justify their place in the classroom.

At the same time, true to her vision of the necessary connection between intellectual inquiry and social activism, Cole built on the tradition of community service and on her personal engagement with social issues to build the bridges to the community (local and global) that she talked about in her inauguration address. She established an International Affairs Center and an Office of Community Service.

When asked about her philosophy of life, Cole says, "The philosophy that really guides me is that I will do well if I can just find ways to do good." She expands that definition: "Doing well, not only means a level of comfort, it means a level of peace, a kind of inner peace. It means moving with a sense of joy. That kind of doing well only comes, I think, when you're doing good."[22]

According to a 1998 study of three exemplary black colleges and universities, "During Johnnetta Cole's presidency, Spelman became a media sensation for its academic excellence, outstanding women students, and enormous success in fund-raising." By the end of her term, the endowment had risen to $156.4 million, the faculty was rated twenty-first among the nation's liberal arts colleges in *U.S. News & World Report*, and the six-year graduation rate was 72 percent, with 78 percent of students coming from forty-five states and twenty-nine foreign countries. The same study concludes that even though Cole thought she was a risky choice when the trustees selected her, "Johnnetta Cole embodied the essence of Spelman College, its focus on excellence and women's leadership."[23]

In sum, Cole arrived at Spelman with little fundraising experience but built on an infrastructure begun by her predecessor and expanded the philanthropic base to realize a vision in which intellectual excellence and social activism are joined. In addition to a record-breaking capital campaign, she raised the national profile of Spelman and increased applications and enrollments at a time when women's colleges and historically black colleges were under siege.

When Cole completed her term at Spelman, she continued to make change in educational and cultural institutions, first at Emory University for three years and then at Bennett College, where she served as president from 2002 to 2007. Unwilling to retire, she combined her love of art and her administrative skills when she became director of the Smithsonian National Museum of African Art in Washington, DC, in 2009, a position she held until March 2017. She is currently principal consultant at Cook Ross, a consulting firm in Silver Springs, Maryland, dedicated to inclusive leadership, and recently was named senior consulting fellow of the Andrew W. Mellon Foundation.

Cole's leadership at Spelman was marked by her effort to read the culture—to understand how and why power relationships and traditions came to be. Her willingness to do the inner work required to unearth her own assumptions and biases was joined to her efforts to understand the college and to make change in a productive way through collaboration. She describes her collaborative style of leadership as creating the very vision of a college collectively: "I don't think we do a particularly good job of this across American higher education. There's certainly no college or university without its vision statement, without its mission statement, or without a strategic plan that's in a great big binder that sits on every bookshelf. But when those activities are taken seriously, done genuinely, you've got a platform for moving forward."

When asked about what gives her the most pleasure as she thinks about her long and distinguished career, she says,

> I rarely go more than a day or so without either encountering a Spelman or Bennett alumna or in some way being reengaged with those two women's colleges. It's just pure joy to be with women who, to use language we used in my era, because they were at a women's college, believed that they could fly. And it's not just encountering these alumnae who are now practicing physicists or artists or teachers or physicians, it's always hearing "And Sister President, I want you to know I started an organization to support girls in my community." To use the language of Mary McLeod Bethune, these are women who don't just climb, they lift others as they climb.[24]

Notes

1 Beverly Guy-Sheftall, "Spelman College," C-SPAN, March 29, 1994, video, https://www.c-span.org/video/?55631-1/spelman-college.

2 Glenn Collins, "Spelman College's First 'Sister President,'" *New York Times*, July 20, 1987, http://www.nytimes.com/1987/07/20/style/spelman-s-college-s -first-sister-president.html.

3 Alison Bernstein and Johnnetta B. Cole, "Johnnetta Cole: Serving by Example," *Change* 19, no. 5 (September–October 1987): 46–55, http://www.jstor.org/ stable/40164667.

4   Johnnetta B. Cole, interview by Phyllis Leffer and Julian Bond, Explorations in Black Leadership, University of Virginia, November 14, 2001, http://www .blackleadership.virginia.edu/interview/cole-johnnetta. Complete transcript available on the project website.

5   Bernstein and Cole, "Johnnetta Cole," 46.

6   Cole, interview by Leffer and Bond.

7   Bernstein and Cole, "Johnnetta Cole," 50.

8   Johnnetta B. Cole, in discussion with the author, January 7, 2018. All direct quotes and statements are taken from this interview unless otherwise noted.

9   Cole, interview by Leffer and Bond.

10 Kimberlé Crenshaw, "Mapping the Margins: Intersectionality, Identity Politics, and Violence against Women of Color," Stanford Law Review 43, no. 6 (July 1991): 1241–1299, https://doi.org/10.2307/1229039.

11 Cole, interview by Leffer and Bond.

12 Ibid.

13 Scott Jaschik, "Spelman Will Admit Transgender Students," Issues in Higher Ed, September 7, 2017, https://www.insidehighered.com/quicktakes/2017/09/ 07/spelman-will-admit-transgender-students.

14 See Paula Giddings, When and Where I Enter: The Impact of Black Women on Race and Sex in America (New York: William Morrow, 1984); and Linda Beatrice Brown, Belles of Liberty: Gender, Bennett College and the Civil Rights Movement (Greensboro, N.C.: Women and Wisdom Foundation, 2013).

15 "Case History: The Spelman College Endowment," Commonfund Institute, March 2009, 3, https://eric.ed.gov/?id=ED559306.

16 In the wake of widely publicized charges of sexual harassment against Bill Cosby, Spelman College discontinued endowed chairs named in his honor and returned relevant funds to the foundation overseeing Cosby philanthropy in 2015. Scott Jaschik, "Spelman Discontinues Cosby Professorship," Inside Higher Ed, July 27, 2015, https://www.insidehighered.com/quicktakes/2015/07/27/ spelman-discontinues-cosby-professorship.

17 "Case History," 3.

18 Johnnetta B. Cole, Conversations: Straight Talk with America's Sister President (New York: Doubleday, 1993), 180.

19 Ibid.

20 Bernstein and Cole, "Johnnetta Cole," 49–50.

21 Carlos Rodriguez, Rita Kirshstein, and Margaret Hale, Creating and Maintaining Excellence: The Model Institutions for Excellence Program, report prepared by the American Institute for Research, May 6, 2005, 40, https://www.air.org/sites/ default/files/downloads/report/MIE_Report_final_0.pdf.

22 Cole, interview by Leffer and Bond.

23 Ursula Wagener and Michael T. Nettles, "It Takes a Community to Educate Students," Change 30, no. 2 (March–April 1998): 18–25.

24 Ibid.

Hanna Holborn Gray and Graduate Education at the University of Chicago

Carol T. Christ

Background

In 1978, when Hanna Holborn Gray became president of the University of Chicago, she began by examining the situation of the university both in relation to its past and traditions and in the broader context of developments in higher education. The situation was not encouraging; 1978 was a difficult economic time, marked by inflation and low market returns (stagflation, as it was called). The real value of federal funding was in decline. The country was in the midst of an energy crisis. Demographic changes—a decline in the numbers of college-age students and an increasing sense of the urgency of increasing student diversity—had an impact on enrollment planning. Academic jobs for PhDs were scarce, and graduate-school enrollments were declining, a fact that motivated concerns about the right size of graduate programs.

The University of Chicago faced particular problems. In 1975, Edward Levi had resigned suddenly as its president to become the U.S. attorney general. His provost, John Wilson, became acting president. After a presidential search failed, Wilson agreed to a three-year term as president on the condition that he would spend minimal time on fundraising and alumni affairs. When Hanna Gray succeeded him as president, the university was struggling with financial distress; its budget was in deficit, a deficit that was projected to increase in the coming years. The value of its endowment had fallen, and the university had just declared the end of a faltering fundraising campaign. Annual fundraising was on the decline. Deferred maintenance needs were acute, and undergraduate applications had fallen, in part due to the lingering effect of political conflicts of the 1960s, in part due to a sense that undergraduate life at Chicago wasn't "fun." The university lacked a budget office and much in the way of a fundraising staff; administrative systems development was minimal. In this rather daunting context, President Gray asked the most fundamental of questions: What should the university aspire to be? She had the intuition that the undergraduate and graduate programs of the university were not in ideal or ideally coherent balance. Important questions needed to be raised about each—and about their relationship. Such questions go to the heart of a university's identity; a president who raises them maladroitly or with a sense that she has already made up her mind about the answers can quickly compromise her ability to lead. Faculty rightfully feel that decisions about academic programs lie in their purview; they themselves must own the questions— questions they believe are important and timely.

Resolution

President Gray was the ideal leader to ask such questions. She grew up in an academic family that gave her an unusually broad and sophisticated experience of academic life. She was born in 1930 in Heidelberg, Germany; her father, Hajo Holborn, was a prominent European historian, and her mother, Annemarie Bettmann, who was Jewish, had a PhD in philology. In 1933, as part of the Nazi effort to discredit and silence liberal and progressive voices in universities, the government dissolved the university at which Professor Holborn taught, the Hochschule für Politik in Berlin, and his position was terminated. He held another position at the University of Berlin, from which he was also terminated. The Holborns decided they needed to leave Germany. They immediately began a period of exile, first in London, then in the United States. Professor Holborn's search for academic work ended with his appointment to the faculty of Yale University in 1934.

Hanna Gray arrived in New Haven with her family at the age of four. She grew up in an academic world, populated extensively with academic refugees from Europe. Her parents were deeply involved in the academic émigré community. Conversations in their living room ranged over many topics: political, international, historical, philosophical. In her memoir, *An Academic Life*, she attests to the impact of this experience: "The large personalities I observed and the debates to which I listened were a significant part of my education."[1] Like her parents, she learned to live in two cultures: the European culture they had brought with them from Germany and the American one they were adopting. This double perspective deeply enriched her understanding of both history and culture.

After attending the Foote School in New Haven and the Sidwell Friends School in Washington, DC, where Hanna's father worked for the Office of Strategic Services during the Second World War, she entered Bryn Mawr for her undergraduate education at the age of fifteen. Alone among the Seven Sisters, Bryn Mawr had had a graduate school from its founding. Its focus on women's intellectual talents and their capacity for serious scholarship reinforced those values from Hanna's own upbringing. She majored in history, with Latin as a secondary area of concentration. After graduation, she went to Oxford for a year on a Fulbright. She then earned her doctorate at Harvard, where she met and married her husband, Charles Montgomery Gray, a fellow graduate student in history, whom she met in a Renaissance history seminar. After completing his doctorate, Charles Gray first taught at Massachusetts Institute of Technology and then was offered a faculty position at the University of Chicago; Hanna followed, convinced she would need to find something else to do because of the nepotism rules in force at the time. She thought about going to law school. Offered a year's fellowship at the Newberry Library, she also did some teaching. In 1961, to her surprise, Chicago's history department offered her an assistant professorship. At that point, women made up only 7 percent of the faculty, with most of the few tenured women holding positions in the School of Social Service Administration.

President Gray's faculty career at the University of Chicago gave her wide acquaintance with the faculty of the university and a deep understanding of its culture. This is how she describes it: "A united community of scholars that understood with total clarity its intellectual mission of pursuing intellectual discovery and learning, open to intellectual ventures that crossed disciplinary lines, proud of sustaining a tradition of vigorous debate, offering unusual freedom to its members to choose their paths of teaching and research, and populated with gifted and interesting students who worked hard and were not afraid to see themselves as budding intellectuals" (181).

Chicago had a distinctive undergraduate core curriculum emphasizing general, cross-disciplinary education taught by a separate teaching faculty; graduate programs were organized by divisions and were relatively independent of one another and from the undergraduate college. In President Gray's early years as a faculty member, she saw two talented leaders (Alan Simpson, the dean of the college, and Edward Levi, the provost, who after Simpson's departure to become president of Vassar appointed himself the interim dean of the college as well) address these structural issues, revising the college's curriculum and bringing the college into closer and better alignment with the graduate school. This process clearly had a shaping influence on President Gray's developing understanding of the particular character of the university, of the complex relationship between its undergraduate college and its graduate programs, and of the character of successful institutional leadership.

An even more decisive issue in developing President Gray's capacity for leadership and understanding of its challenges and satisfactions was her chairing a committee to investigate a controversial appointment case. In 1968, Marlene Dixon, a radical feminist sociologist, was told that her assistant professorship would not be renewed. Wide protests and a sit-in followed. Edward Levi, now president, appointed a committee with Hanna Gray as chair to investigate the circumstances of the case and determine whether its adjudication had been fair and had followed the appropriate process. The committee upheld the decision. Although Dixon's supporters were disappointed by the results, many in the university community praised the work of the committee and Gray's leadership of it.

Gray writes about this experience: "I have never learned so much in so short a time. Nor have I been more absorbed by the task of finding a way through the complexities of ascertaining essential facts or working through differences of opinion and perspective to reach a reasonable and explicable judgment. That process is, indeed, what I later found most compelling in the world of academic administration" (191).

The Dixon committee had made President Gray more visible, and she began to get inquiries about presidential jobs, for which she knew she was not ready. But without aspiring to an administrative career, she had begun to understand its appeal, both in substance and in value. She writes, "I liked chairing meetings, finding ways to move toward consensus, and coming to consequential policy recommendations and actions, and I felt an acute sense of how important it was to maintain the always fragile character of institutions whose missions would be damaged, perhaps irrevocably, were they to become politicized and lose the primary purposes and requisite freedoms that justified their existence" (194).

In 1970, she was offered the position of dean of the College of Arts and Sciences at Northwestern University, a position she accepted and from which she learned the very different dynamics and issues in another university environment and the challenges of change—both how difficult it was to create something new and how hard to eliminate the old.

In 1973, Yale's president, Kingman Brewster, invited Gray to become provost at Yale, beginning the academic year 1974–1975. She had become a fellow of the Yale Corporation in 1970 (Yale's governing body), so she was familiar in general terms with Yale's particular assets and challenges, but the responsibility of serving as provost involved an entirely different level of engagement and responsibility. In 1969, Yale had begun to admit women to its undergraduate college, a change toward which there was still some lingering alumni resentment. Like most universities, Yale was suffering from the stagflation of the 1970s; it had massive deferred maintenance problems, a significant deficit, some weaknesses in the sciences and engineering, a new management school to develop, and serious labor problems. In 1977, Kingman Brewster left to become ambassador to Great Britain, and Hanna was asked to serve as the interim president, simultaneously keeping the provost's job, while a presidential search was being conducted. Although Gray did not believe she was a credible candidate for the presidency, the year was awkward and challenging, both because of all the speculation about the search and whether she was a candidate in it and because of the difficulty of doing both jobs simultaneously.

In 1978, Gray was offered the presidency of the University of Chicago. Her experiences had contributed to her preparation and capacity for the position in consequential ways. She had been a dean, a provost, and a president. She had gotten to know well two other comparable universities whose particular characteristics and challenges could enhance her understanding of the University of Chicago. From her experience as a faculty member, she had a broad and deep knowledge of the university she was about to lead. And she had dealt with the entire range of problems with which universities had been confronted through a difficult decade.

From the time that Gray was appointed dean of Northwestern's College of Arts and Sciences, the media had been interested in her as the first woman in the positions that she held, an interest that surprised and amused her. She notes that she was constantly asked about what it was like to be a woman rather than about her views on higher education (198). By her own account, however, the University of Chicago "often regarded as a conservative institution, had taken a step about which its trustees and faculty seemed not to fuss at all." She continues, "I was never treated as a different species or made to feel that my gender caused alarm" (xi). She then recounts the chairman of the board's introduction of her at her inauguration as the first—and here a long pause—foreign-born president of the university. Gray has consistently represented the fact of her gender as unremarkable. Although she has taken strong stands on gender equity issues, she does not present herself as exceptional because she is a woman. Nonetheless, her career exemplifies the remarkable transformation since the 1960s in the opportunities and assumptions that have shaped women's lives.

When Gray began her appointment as president, intent on asking that most fundamental of questions (What should the university try to be?), she felt confident in what she described and believed as its "essential endowment": its culture, its sense of mission, and its purpose. She believed that Chicago's powerful sense of mission—"its uncompromising intellectual spirit, its insistence on intellectual freedom, its capacity for interdisciplinary discourse and scholarship, its exceptional students, and the breadth and rigor of education they had on offer" (243)—provided a strong foundation from which to launch the fundamental inquiry on which she was intent.

In her memoir, she writes about the temptation, in assuming an executive position, to try to do everything that needs doing right away. She argues that a leader needs a sense of pace and priorities— a sense of what to do at the beginning, and over what length of time, and how to distribute one's goals. She saw the need to listen, even in a university she knew well, "to discover the nature and state of the institutional culture and where it seemed to be heading," to talk with as many people as possible to understand what was on their minds: "their intellectual interests and ideas and hopes for their institution, the quality of the scholarly and scientific work they observed around them, the trends and directions of their disciplines, and the projects that held the most promise in their thinking" (243).

President Gray wanted to raise the most basic of questions about the university. Concerned about declining undergraduate applications, she wanted to assess the character, weight, and size of the undergraduate college. The undergraduate faculty, despite the earlier work of Alan Simpson and Edward Levi, was still somewhat separate from the faculty of the graduate divisions: humanities, social sciences, biological sciences, and physical sciences. These graduate divisions defined the institutional character of the university, but graduate education was in crisis across the nation, and graduate enrollments were in decline. Both of these areas of questioning (the character and size of the undergraduate college and the nature of the graduate program) strike to the heart not just of institutional but of faculty identity. Change in both areas would depend on the faculty engaging those questions as their own and embracing the process of deliberation.

In raising these questions, Gray was aided by what seems a rather baroque faculty governance structure. The sovereign body was the university senate, which was comprised of all tenure-track faculty. It elected fifty-one members to the council of the university senate, the council elected seven members to form the committee of the council of the university senate, and the committee elected the spokesperson of the committee of the council of the university senate. The president chaired monthly meetings of the council, whose minutes were distributed to the entire senate, and biweekly meetings of the committee. This elaborate structure assured extensive consultation on all matters affecting the university as a whole.

In raising the issues that concerned her, Gray took care to present them in the context of national trends and developments. In the context of the changes she was contemplating, she aspired to a high level of transparency, sharing institutional data and going to great efforts to communicate the university's situation by all the means at her disposal. She used the *University of Chicago Record*, which published all commissioned reports; the annual State of the University talks; and annual reports on the budget. She soon added a new and more informal publication, the *Chronicle*. She used the ritual occasions on which the president addresses the community (the annual State of the University report, for example) to speak about what concerned her, to write about what she saw and perceived. She talked to as many faculty members as possible.

As the means of addressing the two major issues of her concern (the undergraduate college and the graduate programs), she appointed two faculty committees. One, chaired by psychologist Norman Bradburn, was charged with considering the future size, composition, and balance of the university. The other, chaired by historian Keith Baker, was charged with surveying and assessing graduate education. Both presented extensive, substantive reports, which were widely debated in the university community. The issues the two committees addressed were of course related, but it was the second, assessing the quality and effectiveness of graduate education, that was the riskier of the two because it seemed to intrude on matters that the departments felt were in their purview. Faculty were anxious about decreasing the number of graduate students. President Gray in part moderated these concerns by meeting extensively with departments to explain the committee's charge and to elicit their views.

The Bradburn Committee's charge also raised alarm. College faculty feared that the special character of the college might be compromised; faculty primarily associated with graduate programs feared a lessened commitment to graduate education and research and worried that President Gray would favor the college. The committee ultimately recommended a tripartite composition for the university: a third of the university should be devoted to undergraduate education, a third to graduate education, and a third to professional education. This composition by thirds involved increasing the size of the college while maintaining the number of students in graduate programs.

The Baker Commission's report on graduate education resulted in even more far-reaching change—change that was nationally influential. President Gray was concerned that university-wide requirements for the PhD were too rigid (a candidate for the degree needed to complete twenty-seven courses) and that financial aid for graduate students was inadequate. Many departments admitted large first-year classes, which they proceeded to weed out; they did not award multiyear fellowships. Dropout rates in the years in which students were writing their dissertations, particularly in the humanities and social sciences, were too high. The commission was charged with answering questions about fellowships, about admissions, about requirements, and about the relative strengths and weaknesses of the four divisions: humanities, social sciences, biological sciences, and physical sciences. Here is how its chair described its task:

> To consider the present state and future state of graduate education
> in the light of its traditional commitment to excellence in teaching
> and research and the current constraints on the organization of
> higher education. . . . Among the issues the commission has been

charged to consider are the assumptions and goals underlying our approaches to graduate education at the University of Chicago and the strengths and weaknesses of our current programs; our policies relating to admissions and aid and our ability to identify, attract and sustain the most promising students; the requirements and length of time expected for the completion of graduate degree programs; the role which graduate students play in research and teaching.[2]

The Baker Commission worked for two years; it collected data and surveyed both current graduate students and those who had been admitted but chose not to come to the university. Like President Gray herself, the commission approached its charge at the highest level of principle: "Given the prevailing sense of crisis in graduate education, this Commission believes that it is imperative that the faculty evaluate its commitment to this traditional responsibility, consider the principles and assumptions on which it rests, and assess the means by which it is being pursued. . . . As faculty members, we must ask ourselves—and be willing to explain to others—what it is we wish to achieve and why. What is the idea of graduate education at this University?"[3]

Although the Baker Commission was motivated by a sense that graduate education across the country was in crisis, it rejected "a strategy of planned shrinkage." It advocated instead "bold initiatives that reconceptualize graduate education more generally."[4] It then proceeded to recommend sweeping changes in graduate education at the University of Chicago. This was the report's genius. In the framework of defending the university's historic commitment to graduate education, the commission recommended many substantive changes. It thus balanced conservative and progressive impulses and achieved significant reform under the banner of maintaining historic commitment.

The commission recommended significant changes in the structure of programs and requirements. Course requirements were reduced by one third; the report stipulated that coursework should normally be limited to two years. It developed a regular schedule of advancement to candidacy. The commission recommended extensive changes in financial aid and in the cost of attendance. Students admitted to candidacy after two years would pay half tuition for the next two years; after three years of residency, students would pay a reduced fee for full-time certification. The commission recommended greatly expanded and systematized financial aid structured by multiyear packages.

The commission was particularly attentive to the isolation that students, particularly in the humanities and social sciences, often experienced when writing their dissertations. It recommended a system of workshops in which students were to present their dissertation research to their fellow students, thus creating a more collegial environment. These dissertation workshops became a national model. The commission also recommended more teaching opportunities for graduate students. This proved to be controversial; there was concern that graduate student instructors would compromise the character of the undergraduate college. However, a variety of teaching opportunities for graduate students were gradually created. Finally, the commission recommended expanding the Career Counseling and Placement Center to offer fuller counseling and assistance for graduate students seeking nonacademic careers.

All these changes pertain to the structure and quality of the graduate student experience; the commission also made a set of recommendations designed to create more a rigorous review of programs. It asked each department to review its own graduate programs in response to the concerns raised in the report, and it recommended a regular system of program reviews, evaluating each department initially on an accelerated schedule of three to five years and thereafter every ten years. It created an advisory structure for graduate students to articulate their concerns and suggestions to the divisions. It encouraged more general and interdisciplinary programs and opportunities for students to cross the lines between graduate and professional programs and, specifically, the establishment of joint graduate professional programs.

The commission based many of its recommendations and proposals on assessments of the four divisions; these assessments accompanied the report. The report was particularly critical of the humanities and the biological sciences, which seemed ripe for reorientation. (These were years of methodological ferment in the humanities; they were also years in which many universities were reorganizing the biological sciences because of the increasing importance of molecular and cell biology.) It recommended a language institute in the humanities, a research institute in the humanities and social sciences, and a mathematics research institute. It recommended a committee be created to determine whether the university should create a department of computer science.

The thirty-five recommendations offered by the Baker Commission in its 109-page report would have a transformative effect on graduate education at the University of Chicago. When President Gray received the report, she published a response, specifying which recommendations she would accept and implement and which the faculty would debate. The faculty, for example, rejected the idea of a joint institute of humanities and social sciences. Here, as with other issues in her presidency, Gray's approach was highly iterative. She typically framed the question, appointed a carefully selected group of faculty to consider it, tried to make the process as transparent as possible, allowed for full faculty deliberation about the recommendations in which she was very much involved, and communicated clearly and extensively about which recommendations she would implement.

The role of the board of trustees in this process was an interesting one. The board understood the tradition and culture of the institution and had great respect for the faculty. President Gray kept them well informed, and they, for the most part, left academic matters to the faculty and the administration.

In her memoir, Gray writes that "preserving the best of tradition while adapting to evolving challenges and vigorously searching out new ones is an essential source of vitality, the most basic work to which academic leaders at every level of the academy are called" (241). Her work on graduate education at the University of Chicago illustrates this balance. It required understanding the larger environment in higher education as well as the particular culture and traditions of the University of Chicago. The late 1970s and early 1980s were difficult years in higher education. The boom years of the 1960s created the expectation that prosperity and expansion were normal, not exceptional. The contraction of the 1970s therefore seemed all the more frustrating. In President Gray's words, faculty "carried in their academic DNA the mentality of growth and its assumptions at a time of increasing constraint" (241). In her inaugural address, she observes that a natural reaction to the troubled environment "would be to turn inward, toward the protection and preservation of present territory, in a mood inhospitable to risk and to creative imagination." She identifies the dangers of postponement ("the refusal to confront uncomfortable questions") and delegation ("the assignment elsewhere of responsibility for what has happened or what needs doing"). She continues, "The greatest danger, large because also least tangible and most wasting, would be to engage in an apparently principled descent to decent mediocrity."[5] These inaugural words are revealing because they show her willingness to ask uncomfortable questions, to accept responsibility for what needs doing. To do this, she framed those questions in the largest way as questions of mission and identity.

Tufts University president emeritus Lawrence Bacow has said that the most fundamental talent of a university leader is taste—taste in problems and taste in people.[6] By this, he means an instinct for institutionally productive and significant questions and recognition of leadership talent in others. Gray had taste in this sense. She understood the national crisis in graduate education. She also understood that it was critical for the University of Chicago to come to terms with this crisis, given how important graduate education was to the university's sense of its distinctive excellence and identity. And she chose leaders in Keith Baker and in members of the commission who were equal to the task and could rise above parochial and disciplinary loyalties to consider the best interests of the institution.

President Gray had a deep understanding of the governance structures of the university that allowed her to use them for her benefit. The multiple meetings that resulted from the nested set of deliberative bodies (the university senate, the council of the university senate, and the committee of the council of the university senate) gave her ample opportunities not only to communicate but to proceed through an iterative mode of decision-making characteristic of her leadership. Most importantly, she trusted the faculty and respected their role; she believed that they were ready to engage the fundamental questions she wanted to ask. She set up a process that allowed them to do so and trusted the result.

President Gray quickly understood how critical transparency of communication would be to any institutional change. Indeed, she multiplied ways of communicating, understanding how important it was to enable the community to absorb and engage the questions and challenges she saw. She was ultimately clear about what she would do and what would be open to debate.

President Gray writes, "The most important task—and this is surely the central task of all academic leadership—was to identify and to keep reviewing an appropriate balance between the university's traditions and committed values on the one hand, and the challenges and opportunities of change on the other" (241). Her leadership of the reform of graduate education at the University of Chicago shows a mastery of this balance. In her inaugural address, President Gray argued that the way to avoid the principled descent to decent mediocrity was "to take the difficult necessary steps to decide on our own principal directions, to concentrate on what we aim to do best, to be willing to define and to make the major choices of internal priority."[7] She was willing not only to do this herself but to lead her community in this process. In doing so, she made the University of Chicago a much stronger institution, strengthening both the undergraduate college and graduate education at the university.

Notes

1 Hanna Gray, *An Academic Life* (Princeton, N.J.: Princeton University Press, 2018), 68. Page references for all further quotations will be given in parentheses in the text.

2 Quoted from Hanna Gray, "The State of the University 1980," *University of Chicago Record* 14, no. 6 (December 1980): 214.

3 "Don't Cut Graduate Programs," *University of Chicago Magazine* 75, no. 1 (September 1982): 26.

4 Ibid., 25.

5 Hanna Gray, "The Inaugural Address," *University of Chicago Record* 12, no. 8 (December 11, 1978): 164.

6 Lawrence Bacow, seminar, Berkeley, Calif., April 19, 2016.

7 Gray, "Inaugural Address," 165.

Decolonializing across Broadway

The Barnard Presidency of Judith R. Shapiro

Karen R. Stubaus

Background

Judith Shapiro is said to have been a transformative president for Barnard College.[1] All the important markers are there: Under her watch, applications more than doubled in number and increased in quality, making Barnard the most selective women's college in the country by the end of her time in office. The college's endowment skyrocketed, as did the number of alumnae making gifts. While she was president, Barnard embarked on several significant building and renovation projects, culminating in the construction of the Diana Center, a stunning multipurpose structure on Broadway. The reputation of the college was significantly better on the day she left than it had been on the day she arrived.

Shapiro served as the sixth president of Barnard College from 1994 through 2008, the first of Barnard's presidents to have been educated in New York City public schools. Majoring in history at Brandeis (and singing in local coffee houses with a folk group called The Colliers[2]), Shapiro graduated magna cum laude and went on to earn her PhD in anthropology at Columbia University.[3] Her anthropological training never left her. "There's a way in which, when you're an anthropologist, you're always an anthropologist," she notes. "It's a way of looking at the world." Quite aptly, her research focused on gender differences, social organization, cultural theory, and missionization.[4]

Shapiro's first appointment was to the Department of Anthropology at the University of Chicago in 1970, where she was the first woman member of the faculty. It was not a happy time. "I had no women among the faculty who taught me," she notes. "At Chicago, I was young, insecure, and not established. I hadn't finished my dissertation. Everybody in my department was a male, senior faculty member. It was intimidating."[5]

Fortunately, the Chicago phase of her career did not last long. In 1975, she accepted an appointment as an assistant professor of anthropology at Bryn Mawr, where in a few years, she was to meet Mary Patterson McPherson, president of Bryn Mawr College from 1978 to 1997. Shapiro speaks of McPherson with great warmth and affection; she was, and remains, an important person in her life—a close colleague, friend, and mentor. In fact, Shapiro credits McPherson with putting her on the path that would eventually lead her to the Barnard presidency: "Pat McPherson asked me to be acting dean of the undergraduate college at Bryn Mawr. It was a pivotal moment. At the time, I was a senior faculty member and chairman of the anthropology department. It was a low-risk way to try being a college administrator, and it was not a difficult decision to make." A year later, McPherson appointed Shapiro to provost, a position she would hold for eight years until Barnard called her to be its new president.[6]

The institution Shapiro led for fourteen years describes itself today as "a distinguished leader in higher education, offering a rigorous liberal arts foundation to young women whose curiosity, drive, and exuberance set them apart."[7] Understanding its geography is, and always has been, an essential component in understanding Barnard and its place in the world, including its psychological place in the world.

Both Barnard and the rest of Columbia University, with which Barnard is in partnership (as Shapiro describes the relationship), are located in Upper Manhattan at 116th Street and Broadway. In fact, Broadway is the physical and psychological dividing line, with Barnard occupying four acres on one side and Columbia occupying nine times that on the other. Today Barnard is "a diverse intellectual community in a unique learning environment that provides the best of all worlds: small, intimate classes in a collaborative liberal arts setting dedicated to the advancement of women with the vast resources of Columbia University just steps away—in the heart of vibrant and electric New York City." The Upper Manhattan location is touted now; in the past, it presented a bit of a problem for both Barnard and Columbia, one that fed into the question of coeducation and Barnard's very existence.[8]

The 1970s saw the demise of many single-sex colleges, particularly women's colleges. Barnard, like many other similar institutions, was under threat. To make matters more precarious, the New York City of the 1970s was not the New York City of today. Crime was a major issue. Upper Manhattan was underserved, somewhat unpleasant, and not an area that enough would-be college students or their parents found attractive. Columbia College's qualified applicant pool was fewer in number than what it needed for the university's fiscal solvency. Barnard was right across the street. A merger with (or hostile takeover of) Barnard could be the solution to their fiscal problems and one that was in keeping with the national rise in coeducation.[9]

Ultimately, it was Ellen Futter who faced down Columbia and preserved Barnard as a semiautonomous women's college with its own faculty, its own land, its own endowment, and its own board of trustees. Futter was appointed acting president and then president of the college in 1980 and 1981, respectively, following the dismissal of Jacquelyn Mattfeld, who had served as president for just four years and who apparently was not equipped to effectively resist Columbia's acquisitive instincts. She was dismissed in 1980 by the board and replaced by Futter, the board's youngest member.[10]

Futter's appointment as acting president and then president "after a decade of tense relations with Columbia" was counterintuitive to some board members. As noted by Barnard historian Robert McCaughey, "The appointment of Ellen V. Futter as acting president, two months shy of her thirtieth birthday, surprised everyone outside the Barnard board—and quite possibly some within. Faculty representatives to the board learned of her selection in the *New York Times*."[11] Futter was judged to be extremely young to be assuming the presidency, even on an acting basis. In addition, although she was indeed a Barnard graduate, she was a transfer student, having spent her first two undergraduate years at the University of Wisconsin. To make matters worse, her graduate training was not in a traditional academic discipline but rather in law, and her professional experience to date was as a corporate attorney. The only possible point of reassurance for the skeptical was that her appointment was to last for only one year while a search was conducted—at the end of which, she would return to practicing law.

However, Futter's appointment did make sense along several lines. Her relative youth might prove to be a positive with regard to the relationship between the office of the president and the Barnard student body, which had been suboptimal during Mattfeld's time. And although she was not an academic, she possessed an enormous amount of local and institutional knowledge that would be of use to any president of the college. She had been born in New York City and raised on Long Island. Her father was a graduate of both Columbia College and Columbia Law School and had served as president of the Columbia College Alumni Association. She graduated magna cum laude from Barnard in 1971 and had been a student leader. Like her father, she earned her law degree from Columbia. And perhaps most importantly, she had served on Barnard's board for eight years before being named acting president.[12]

Thus it was that Ellen Futter was president of Barnard College when Columbia College determined to go coed. Shortly after her appointment in 1981, the board authorized her to discuss coeducation with Columbia University's president, Michael Sovern, who had also been Futter's law school professor and dean. Those discussions confirmed the absence of an extant agreement that could prevent Columbia College from admitting women; and Barnard, with its separate trustees, endowment, faculty, and library, was not interested in a merger. In December of that year, President Sovern informed Futter of the university's decision to permit Columbia College to admit women for the fall of 1983, making Columbia the last college in the Ivy League to do so.[13]

The *New York Times* coverage as the first class of Columbia College women arrived on Morningside Heights that August was a bit worrying if read through a Barnard lens:

It was a day of celebration at Columbia, with few alumni or students criticizing the change, and with college administrators saying the decision to admit women had resulted in the most talented freshman class ever.

But across Broadway, at Barnard College, the mood was more reserved. . . . Barnard refused to merge with its brother school last year, and officials conceded they might lose many promising applicants.[14]

A *New York Times* article articulated prevailing attitudes. Young women who had chosen Columbia, even if accepted at Barnard as well, explained their decision: "My dad went to Columbia, my brother went to Columbia, and it was only fitting that I should go to Columbia," said seventeen-year-old Laurie Gershon of Westport, Connecticut. She and her roommate, Jocelyn Rause, eighteen, of Pittsburgh, were comparing record collections: "My Mom went to Barnard, but she wanted me to come here, too," said Miss Gershon, who added she had also been accepted at Barnard but had chosen Columbia because, in her words, "I think a Columbia degree will have more prestige in the long run."[15]

And a Columbia College man weighed in: "The women who now choose Barnard are making that choice because they think they'll thrive in an all-female environment, not be hindered by men," said Mark Simon, a senior majoring in history at Columbia and the president of the student admissions committee. "Columbia women, on the other hand, are not afraid to compete." But Barnard held its ground: "A women's college is not just a building or a campus, it's an attitude, a philosophy of education," said R. Christine Royer, director of admissions at Barnard. "Here everyone just assumes that a woman can do everything and be everything she wants to do and be. I think the women who recognize this will make the wise choice." And then, an ominous note: "The problem Barnard faces over the next few years . . . is to find those women."[16]

Applications to Barnard did indeed dip for a time but eventually rebounded. As the first Barnard president faced with coeducation across Broadway, Futter worked hard to ensure the college's long-term future under the new world order, initiating a major fundraising campaign, leading a significant revision of the curriculum, and in 1986, making the risky decision to move forward with the building of a new and much-needed residence hall that would solidify Barnard as a primarily residential college even though the funding for it had not yet been identified.[17]

This was the Barnard that Shapiro took over in 1994, a little over ten years after Columbia went coed. It was still a women's college and apparently stable, but not without its challenges. Of her earliest days at Barnard, Shapiro notes, "I hadn't planned to become a college president, but when I met with the search committee, I fell in love with the place." Shapiro describes that love affair as being fed by the fact that Barnard was a women's college; the fact that it was located in New York, where she had grown up; and the fact that she had earned her PhD in anthropology right across Broadway at Columbia. Given all that, she says, "It just felt right."

Even though the existential threat had presumably been met and overcome more than a decade before, a close friend asked Shapiro along the way if she would want to come to Barnard if it were to merge with Columbia. Shapiro gave a resounding no. She explains, "To me, there was never any possibility of merging with Columbia. In fact, while I was president of Barnard, I worked hard every day to decolonialize the relationship between Barnard and Columbia. To make Barnard—its faculty, students, and staff—feel strong in relation to Columbia." That comment, spoken in the language of the anthropologist Shapiro was and is, holds the key to the transformative nature of her presidency.

Decolonialize. How do you operationalize the concept in an academic environment? How do you make it real, and how do you make it redound to the benefit of Barnard's faculty, students, and staff?

Resolution

To begin with, you don't do it alone. Shapiro hastens to note that she was aided and abetted by many in the college—most notably by Elizabeth S. Boylan, who Shapiro appointed provost and dean of the faculty in 1995, and Dorothy Denburg, Barnard alumna and already beloved by students in her role as dean of the college when Shapiro arrived on the scene. The three were a tight team, and together they worked with focused intentionality on the decolonialization project.

Boylan recalls what was confronting them in 1995:

> We were faced with certain realities at the time I joined the team.
> The realities included the fact that there were many more women
> applying to Columbia, and some had higher SAT scores than
> the applicant pool at Barnard. Ellen [Futter] had rescued the college
> from this time of existential threat and put it on a course of inde-
> pendence in a principled way. It was a risky move. Judith [Shapiro]
> came in and was hired to solidify and stabilize the college's identity
> and prestige as well as the competitiveness of the faculty and its
> academic reputation. That is what I understood my main objectives
> were as I began in the summer of 1995.
>
> Having learned some of the recent history of the Barnard-
> Columbia relationship, I found that there was a not an unsurpris-
> ing amount of arrogance and maybe you could even say disdain . . .
> from the leadership at Columbia, as one could say befits an Ivy
> League university . . . that was a very important dynamic. So they
> had their own inner demons. And to have this independent college
> who stood up for itself sometimes and was sometimes feisty and
> was a bother, and for it to be a women's college headed by all
> these women administrators—you know it was hard for some
> of these folks to deal with.[18]

Nevertheless, the decolonializing commenced as soon as Shapiro became president. The work was quiet, collegial, and often subterranean but also extremely intentional, strategic, and persistent. And it was carried out in all arenas, with Columbia's leadership and board, as well as with its faculty, students, and staff.

In keeping with Shapiro's personality and approach to life, very often there was a bit of humor involved. When, for instance, a Barnard student would complain to her that they were getting attitude from Columbia students about how much better they were, Shapiro would tell them, "Look, if you start defending Barnard, you've lost the argument. It's about them. They have status anxiety because they're worried they're not as good as Harvard, Princeton, or Yale."

Decolonializing the faculty at Barnard was a somewhat different matter. The problem was that some Barnard faculty were, or sought to be, more associated with Columbia. It did not take Shapiro long to notice that the faculty were listing Columbia, not Barnard, on their publications. This would not do. "Now look," she would say to the offending faculty member, "I see you are giving Columbia as your affiliation. Let me point out that the glory is not to Columbia—the glory is to you. So we need *you* to confer the glory on Barnard, which, by the way, is paying your salary." Everyone would then laugh, but they got it. And they started complying. Barnard started getting more visibility and more respect. But as Barnard's president, Shapiro's primary charge was to change some minds at the top.

George Rupp had been president of Columbia University for just one year when Shapiro arrived at Barnard in 1994. He would remain in that position until 2002, when he was succeeded by Lee Bollinger. Shapiro speaks with great warmth and fondness of her time with Rupp. "I grew to be very fond of George. I came to value him very much as a colleague, and we worked very well together," Shapiro notes. But initially, Rupp had certain preconceived notions about the academic qualifications of Barnard students relative to those at Columbia. As Shapiro puts it, "In my early years, George wasn't convinced how wonderful Barnard was." That view was shared by a number of Columbia administrators, particularly those who had been at the university for some time.[19] Shapiro suggested that they actually look at some data and commissioned an analysis of all Columbia and Barnard courses and grades, as well as student distribution across the majors.

The results: Barnard women and Columbia men tracked identically; the data indicated that there was no statistically significant difference in the performance of the two groups, even though the average incoming SAT scores were higher at Columbia than at Barnard. Further, if one compared Columbia women and Columbia men, the women slightly outperformed the men, allowing Shapiro to charge Rupp, with some glee, that Columbia was "doing affirmative action for men." In addition, there were more women majoring in the natural sciences and math at Barnard than men with those majors at Columbia, which Shapiro also pointed out to Rupp.

Early on, Shapiro also aggressively addressed the language used to describe the Barnard-Columbia relationship. From her knowledge of anthropological linguistics, Shapiro knew that the language used to describe a group can be just as important in framing a conversation or altering a perception as the production of data sets. When she arrived at Barnard in 1994, the term used to describe the relationship between Barnard College and Columbia University was *affiliation*. Shapiro insisted that it be described instead as a partnership, putting front and center the equal status of the parties involved.[20] Part of the Shapiro legacy is the fact that the relationship to this day is so described: *"The partnership between Barnard College and Columbia University is unique in American higher education*. Both institutions benefit from this historic relationship [that] allows each to leverage the assets and experience of the other—in classrooms, on the athletic fields, in extracurricular activities and clubs, and through many shared resources. . . . At the same time, Barnard is legally and financially independent; has a separate administration, faculty, and admissions office; sets its own policies; and maintains its own endowment and fundraising."*[21] However, in spite of Shapiro's efforts, Rupp would at times use the word *anomalous* to describe the Barnard-Columbia linkage. "I got him to understand," Shapiro notes, "that a linguistic anthropologist would call that a 'negative polarity item.' I suggested to him that he might want to use the word 'unique' instead. I didn't try to push him as far as 'uniquely wonderful.'"

In order to most effectively decolonialize the relationship, Shapiro knew that she had to do more than change some minds at the very top: she had to have the full participation—and confidence—of the faculty. That's where Liz Boylan came in. The ultimately successful attitude-altering strategy Boylan and Shapiro hit upon was to quietly but proactively, and with great intentionality, build relationships and alliances across Broadway. Shapiro's focus was at the presidential and board levels, while Boylan interfaced with her counterparts at Columbia—in the early years, primarily Jonathan Cole as Columbia's provost. As Boylan puts it,

> It was all about relationship building with the counterparts in Columbia—in whatever field or office. Usually in any given program area, there would be one person at Barnard and a host of people on the Columbia side, so the asymmetry in faculty size mattered. But the relationships mattered a lot, and we were very intentional about maintaining and cultivating them. Increasingly, that paid off with a greater degree of reciprocity, so when they had a vacancy or when they were thinking about how they were going to move forward, it was not a total afterthought or never-thought to include Barnard; it became "Oh, yes, Barnard is part of this community and needs to be consulted. It might even be a resource we can use for mutual benefit."[22]

Boylan's achievements in the academic realm were subtle but extremely important and were often achieved in concert with Denburg. With regard to the curriculum, many of the formal and informal barriers Barnard students who sought to take certain Columbia courses and majors had faced in the past were greatly eased, giving them access on a par with that of Columbia students.

In the critical area of faculty tenure and promotion, several small but important changes were negotiated, providing Barnard with greater input into the tenure and promotion processes for their own faculty. One of Boylan's earliest victories was to successfully renegotiate the text of the letter sent to outside tenure reviewers. Upon assuming her new position, Boylan thought some changes were needed. Accordingly, she rewrote the letter, thinking that, as Barnard's provost, she had control over this part of the process for her own faculty. It turned out she did not, as it was stipulated in the intercorporate agreement. But rather than simply retreat and accept the canonical text, which had not been altered, Boylan persisted. In the end, her new language was accepted—a small but hugely important victory.

Similar outcomes were achieved in other areas of the tenure and promotion process. Barnard faculty tenure cases were governed by the Columbia provost's office. The process called for an ad hoc committee of five faculty: two tenured Barnard faculty, two tenured Columbia faculty not in the candidate's discipline, and one faculty member from outside the university. All five members of the ad hoc committee were selected by the Columbia provost. Although the written processes were not changed while Shapiro and Boylan were in office, Boylan notes that over time, through persistent and collegial relationship building, she was able to exert much more influence over who the members of the ad hoc committees would be for Barnard tenure candidates than had previously been the case. Boylan notes, "Our increased influence was based on trust and respect and honoring a more coequal relationship."[23]

Perhaps most important in the faculty realm, the academic judgment of the Shapiro-Boylan administration quickly came to be trusted by Columbia's academic leadership, with the result being that in most cases, the Barnard view of which faculty to hire, tenure, and promote prevailed. Shapiro, with justifiable pride, reports that "in all my years at Barnard, a total of maybe three cases that Barnard went yes on went down at Columbia, and in two of those, they eventually deferred to our decision." Decolonialization at work.

While Shapiro and Boylan were increasing Barnard's stature in their respective realms, Denburg, dean of the college, was attending to the extant issues in student affairs. A Barnard alumna herself, Denburg had been appointed dean by Shapiro's predecessor, Futter; it was a role she was to maintain throughout Shapiro's presidency. Denburg states, "Judith encouraged the administrators who worked with students to take a more aggressive stance and not view ourselves as in any way subservient to Columbia."[24] Shapiro assisted Denburg in asserting Barnard's equal status by providing the funding to enable Barnard to contribute more than its fair share to some of the collaborative student programming with Columbia. Denburg notes this was done to make Barnard "less of a minority stakeholder and thus feel—and be—less dependent upon Columbia's largesse. At the same time," she adds, "[Shapiro] was adamant about our maintaining autonomy over student services in ways that supported our mission as a women's college, even when it meant duplicating budgetary lines and structuring student services in a way that might seem redundant." The result was that "the student government presidents felt more empowered; they were more confident in their dealings with their Columbia counterparts."[25]

There is no more striking physical manifestation of Shapiro's determination to increase Barnard's stature within the Columbia community than the Diana Center, a dramatic multipurpose structure on Broadway. Within a month of its opening, Barnard students had "embraced The Diana Center and made it their own,"[26] but even more importantly, it was the first space on the Barnard campus that Columbia University students actively sought out.

When Shapiro arrived at Barnard in 1994, the campus was already engaged in an extensive two-year space-allocation study. That study documented what many already knew to be true: that Barnard's existing physical plant was woefully inadequate for the college's current curriculum, programs, and activities—much less for any additions or expansions that might be contemplated. "The central problem, of course, was that we were a four-acre campus, and there was a huge space crunch," notes Shapiro.

Shapiro was a very hands-on participant in the conceptualization and development of the Diana, as it came to be called, and delighted in the experience from beginning to end. "I was very, very involved," she says, then continues,

> I learned a huge amount—it was one of the major experiences I got to have as president. We wanted it to be a student center but to include other things as well. There was an enormous amount of conversation about what would go into the new building—what would work out best for the campus overall. The level of campus-wide community involvement in the planning for the building was extraordinary. Liz [Boylan] worked extensively with the faculty and Dorothy [Denburg] with the students. We discussed everything. This kind of participation is not always the case when colleges and universities undertake capital projects—far from it!

Designed by the noted architectural firm Weiss/Manfredi and named for Barnard alumna Diana Touliatou Vagelos, Barnard class of 1955, the Diana is a 98,000-square-foot mixed-use building that includes architecture and painting studios, a five-hundred-seat performance space, a black-box theater, a café, a dining room, a reading room, classrooms, faculty offices, and exhibition galleries. With Shapiro's leadership evident, its very design, conceptualized as a vertical campus quad, encourages collaboration between and among diverse constituencies and disciplines, breaking down silos and separations not only within the Barnard community but between Barnard and Columbia.[27]

But the most important thing about the Diana, in the end, was not evident until it opened in 2010, about eighteen months after Shapiro had stepped down as president. Dorothy Denburg says it best:

> If you hold that the redefinition of the relationship with Columbia was the pivotal factor of Judith's presidency, the building of the Diana concretized that, because once the Diana opened, there was a big shift in how Columbia and Barnard students related to one another. Suddenly, Barnard had a facility that drew Columbia students to our side of the street, and so even in that small way, the symbolism socially was very important.
>
> The Diana Center created this big sense of pride for the Barnard students. For instance, suddenly the Columbia students were coming across Broadway for undergraduate architecture courses in the Diana's beautiful new studios and clamoring to do other things on the Barnard campus as well instead of the other way around, as it had historically been. It was huge.[28]

Shapiro set out in 1994 as the new president of Barnard to decolonialize the relationship with Columbia. And by the time she left in 2008, she and her team had succeeded along many fronts. As Boylan puts it, "By the time Judith left, there was a change in the way that people talked about the Barnard-Columbia relationship. At the beginning of Judith's tenure, the Barnard College faculty meetings were consumed by problems. By the end, we were primarily talking about opportunities. That's how Judith and I talked and how we actually ran our lives and saw the future."[29]

Shapiro herself describes the changes she wrought:

By the time I left in 2008, I think what you saw in the context of the Columbia relationship is that you had a group of students who had a much greater sense of pride in their institution and in being Barnard women.

And my sense is also that the faculty had a greater sense of attachment to the college and just a greater sense of pride in being here. Part of it was the context in which I got them to use Barnard instead of Columbia as their affiliation. And the whole culture around the ad hoc tenure and promotion process—I think they just felt more respected, and they felt entitled not to be disrespected by their Columbia colleagues.

Insofar as both faculty and students don't feel that they're in Columbia's shadow in some way, they have more and more a sense of their own value, which is great.

Notes

1 "Past Leaders of the College," Barnard College, Columbia University, accessed April 13, 2020, https://barnard.edu/college-leadership/past-presidents.

2 The singing continued. As president, Shapiro serenaded current students, alumnae, and many others. Today Barnard offers "an educational experience that combines small, intimate classes in a collaborative setting dedicated to women with the vast resources of a major research university." "The Academic Experience," Barnard College, Columbia University, accessed April 20, 2020, https://barnard.edu/academic-experience.

3 Judith Shapiro, in discussion with the author, June 11, 2018. All direct quotes and statements are taken from this interview unless otherwise noted.

4 "Judith Shapiro, President Barnard College," *Education Update* 44, no. 2 (March 2002), http://www.ascd.org/publications/newsletters/education-update/archived-issues.aspx.

5 Ibid.

6 Ibid.

7 "Past Leaders of the College."

8 Ibid.; Elizabeth S. Boylan, in discussion with the author, August 15, 2018.

9 Boylan, discussion.

10 "Past Leaders of the College."

11 Bob McCaughey, "Ellen V. Futter—Biographical Outline," *Columbia Blogs*, July 24, 2017, http://blogs.cuit.columbia.edu/ram31/documents/6-tough -times-depression-war-other-distractions/deans-presidents/ellen-v-futter -biographical-outline/.

12 Ibid.

13 Ibid.; notes from May 14, 2014.

14 Lisa Belkin, "First Coed Class Enters Columbia College," *New York Times*, August 30, 1983, https://nyti.ms/29QfN2F.

15 Ibid.

16 Ibid.

17 "Past Leaders of the College." Also see McCaughey, "Ellen V. Futter."

18 Boylan, discussion.

19 Ibid.

20 Ibid. It should be noted that the formal agreement between the institutions is referred to as an affiliation.

21 "An Education for Tomorrow," Barnard College, https://www.barnard.edu (emphasis added).

22 Boylan, discussion.

23 Ibid.

24 Dorothy Denburg, in discussion with the author, August 29, 2018.

25 Ibid.

26 "The Diana Center," *Barnard News*, March 31, 2010, https://barnard.edu/ headlines/diana-center.

27 "Diana Center Opens at Barnard College," *Detail*, April 2, 2010, https://www .detail-online.com/article/diana-center-opens-at-barnard-college-14323/.

28 Denburg, discussion.

29 Boylan, discussion.

President Regina Peruggi of Kingsborough Community College

Transformative Leadership and Student Success

Jacquelyn Litt

> CUNY's community colleges have assumed the role of the new Ellis Island for those seeking an opportunity to improve their lives and the lives of their families in New York City. We are the actual and metaphorical gateway to the American dream for thousands of New Yorkers.
>
> —Regina Peruggi, testimony to the New York State Board of Regents, December 2012

Background

Dr. Regina Peruggi, an award-winning and distinguished leader in higher education, served as president of Marymount Manhattan College from 1990 through 2001 and Kingsborough Community College (KCC) of the City University of New York (CUNY) from 2004 through 2013.

This chapter examines Peruggi's tenure at KCC to highlight leadership in a sector of the higher education landscape that is little studied and relatively undervalued. The data are drawn largely from an interview by the author with Peruggi in July 2018 as well as from published reports on the college, media content, and evaluations conducted by private research organizations.

Peruggi's appointment as president of KCC marked a return to an institution she knew well. She started at CUNY in 1974 and moved into leadership in academic affairs ten years later. From 1990 through 2001, she served as the first lay president of Marymount Manhattan College. Her educational background prepared her for top leadership positions. She received a BA in sociology from the College of New Rochelle, an MBA from the Stern School of Business at New York University, and an EdD in higher education administration from Teachers College, Columbia University. With the exception of serving as president of the Central Park Conservancy from 2001 through 2004, she has served higher education for nearly four decades.

Peruggi believes deeply in the value of education to improve lives, especially at the community college level. Her life's mission, and North Star, was motivated by her commitment to serving the public good, a calling she discovered through her own education. Reflecting on her youth during a time of social change and activism in the country, she states, "I was in high school and college during the sixties and was very influenced by the Kennedy era during which time there was a tremendous emphasis on being involved in public service. In addition, the education I received in high school and college was also very value focused and emphasized not just getting a job or career but doing something that would make a difference for your fellow man."[1]

Peruggi's career at KCC spanned the decades-long changes in higher education, particularly at the community college level. The college sector itself has its roots in the early twentieth century yet has experienced both ups and downs in recognition and support. In 1950, the first significant expansion brought the number of community colleges up to 250 in the nation. By 1970, the country counted 650 community colleges. By 2013, the number had nearly doubled to 1,200.

New York State initially lagged behind nationwide trends but soon caught up. In 1970, the state operated forty-five community colleges, including KCC, which was established in 1963 as part of the City University of New York. KCC is now one of six community colleges in the CUNY system, the nation's largest urban university.[2] Yet community colleges in New York State were among the most expensive in the nation. Until the establishment of New York's Excelsior Scholarships in 2017, which mandated free tuition for residents who earn up to a specific income cap, Kingsborough students paid more than $3,000 per year in tuition and fees.

During Peruggi's tenure, community colleges were emerging in public and legislative discourse as a new channel for addressing problems of literacy, financial stability, and the gap between educational attainment and the need for skilled labor. Peruggi explains the relative invisibility of the sector until then:

> Community colleges at the time were sort of an undiscovered gem. They had never really come to the fore. [President] Obama and [Vice President] Biden really brought them up [through the American Graduation Initiative]. Before that, they were there but kind of under the radar. And in New York City, they were nowhere to be found. . . . Nobody knew about them. They thought they were junior colleges. They were like the place for people who didn't make it. In New York, everybody used to call it King's Junior—"What is this, the junior college?" They didn't have a clue.[3]

Kingsborough today offers a wide array of associate degree programs, ranging from traditional majors in the liberal arts to accounting, fashion design, early childhood education, and mental health human services, which are more oriented toward professional development. To serve its broad and diverse student body, which now numbers fifteen thousand students (more than half of whom attend full time), KCC also offers courses in English as a foreign language, college career advancement services, a center for career development and experiential learning, and an honors program. By the end of Peruggi's tenure at KCC, she led a staff of eight hundred and an annual operating budget of nearly $60 million in 2012.[4]

Approximately half of undergraduate students nationwide attend a community college. These colleges now serve as the gateway to higher education for those who need remedial education, have low financial flexibility, are employed parents, or are low-income and minority students.[5] Throughout the last century, associate degrees have been credited with elevating household standards of living. In 2012, for example, family households headed by individuals with only a high school degree were more likely to bring in an income too low to satisfy basic housing, food, and health needs. This compares to 8 percent of households headed by a college graduate. Community colleges have also been heralded as essential to filling the workforce needs for skilled labor and platforms for movement to the bachelor's degree.[6]

Yet student persistence and graduation rates at community colleges are low. According to a report from the education and social policy research organization Manpower Demonstration Research Corporation (MDRC), fewer than 40 percent of all students who entered public two-year colleges in 1995–1996 earned a degree.[7] The costs of attendance in both tuition and lost income, students' caregiving and employment obligations, transportation problems, and the high percentage who require remedial education present other challenges to community college presidents whose goal is to retain and graduate their students.[8] These challenges rose to the fore in Peruggi's presidency, to which we now turn.

Peruggi was the first woman appointed president of Kingsborough Community College since the college's founding in 1963. Although Peruggi does not reference gender, she followed six permanent and interim male deans who held the position. In her early years at CUNY, Peruggi had soared up the ranks through appointments and increased responsibilities in academic affairs units, during which she focused on programs for continuing education, literacy, and faculty development and on partnerships with industry, labor unions, and business. About her return to CUNY as KCC president in 2004, she recalls, "I was at CUNY for so long. I started at CUNY in 1974. I left there in '90. I was at Marymount [Manhattan College] eleven years. Then the [Central] Park [Conservancy] for three [years]. And then they actually recruited me to come back."

Peruggi's long-term relationships at CUNY served her well. As she explains, "I knew all the characters. . . . I had a leg up because everybody coming into the CUNY bureaucracy can get eaten up. . . . It's like a shark tank in there. I had known most of these people for years already, so it was easy for me to come back in there, and they didn't give me a hard time because I had good relationships."

Good relationships, developed through her skill and intelligence, brought Peruggi to the presidency and fostered her success. Peruggi used her knowledge of the politics and players at CUNY to her advantage: "I knew who I could get money from and who I couldn't and who would leave me alone." Her long-standing experience at CUNY similarly empowered her to take stands an outsider could not. As she recalls,

> I remember when I came back to CUNY being at a meeting, and it was so frustrating. I remembered saying in public at a meeting that the only disappointing thing about coming back to CUNY after being away for thirteen years was that they still haven't figured out how to articulate to community colleges and senior colleges and they still couldn't figure out what to do with teacher education, and I said that's depressing. I've been away thirteen years and we're still talking about this crap. You know, we put people on the moon in less time, and we can't figure this out?

Peruggi was bolstered by her sponsors who recruited her to both of her presidencies, relationships in current and prior positions, friendships, and her awareness of having a strong reputation at CUNY. Despite these connections and her reputation, she was simultaneously aware of her marginal status in what she called the "boy's club" of CUNY leadership. She states, "I think it's changing, but the first time I was [at CUNY], there was definitely a boy's club, and every decision was [made] over at a poker game on Friday. . . . And even when I came back the second time, there was A; there was B; the deputy chancellor, he had C—and they always had a woman in academic affairs, and they'd always keep that person out. They ran the place. D was the legal counsel. He was in the cabal. It was all still run by men."

Peruggi also notes that she was not included in university-wide decision-making. In some ways, the best she could hope for was to be left alone to carry out her mission at Kingsborough without interference: "I did a lot of good work, you know. And you know, if you do a lot of good work, they leave you alone."

Peruggi faced numerous infrastructure challenges when she returned as president. The registration system inhibited students' chances for graduation. The remedial educational system worked against student retention and graduation. The enrollment management system was not set up to prepare for or handle course planning. On top of all this, she encountered a relatively disconnected student body, a lack of donor base and low alumni engagement, and an entrenched and dispirited faculty and staff. "KCC was going," she said. "It was just going. . . . It just had no life. People were zombified, I thought. . . . They'd been there for so many years. They always did everything the same [way]."

She attributed some of the problems to the outgoing president, who "had been very vindictive if things went awry. . . . He was nasty to [the staff]. He told them they were backward. He got into big fights with these folks on email." Peruggi decided that a wake-up call was in order: "There was a lot of talent, but they were all just there. And they were . . . not intimidated but constrained because of the kind of leadership they had for so many years that was so dominant. They needed to feel empowered. And I thought the first thing that was needed was to wake them up and say, 'Hey, you're really smart people. You know how to do this. You have a good place here. It's running really well. It runs like a finely oiled machine.'"

Peruggi took on the registration system as a first test case. Her goals were to improve the student experience and build trust among her employees. In discussions with faculty and staff, she quickly learned that students were not well served with the current registration system. Through new data collection, she identified that students were registering without appropriate guidance about which classes they needed to take. This was particularly significant for the many students who needed remedial classes—those who would register, for example, for a history class when they couldn't read.

Tackling student morale was another priority. Like most commuter-based community colleges, KCC students are employed or have family obligations, leaving them unable to spend time on campus outside of their assigned class period. Forging ties and peer relationships can be challenging. Yet as Peruggi knew, these factors are positively related to persistence. Addressing the student experience required affirmative actions and new initiatives. Peruggi instituted a party for accepted students in the spring prior to the beginning of the academic year. The reaction among the staff was "We accept everybody." Yet Peruggi insisted, "These kids don't need to know that . . . they need to feel good." She also invited parents "so that they felt like they were going to college. Not like they were failures."

Perhaps one of the largest challenges was the absence of a donor base and no alumni connections or effective college board. When asked to identify her donor base at Kingsborough, Peruggi said, "Nobody. It had no money at all except city money. When I worked at the Central Park Conservancy, I wouldn't sign a [thank-you] letter for under one thousand dollars. At King's, if you send me ten bucks, I write you a little note at the bottom [of the standard thank-you letter]."

Peruggi attributed the absence of donor funding at KCC to a past president who served for over twenty years. In her view, he was "a master politician and has his hooks into everyone at the state level. And he never raised a dime other than public money. And he didn't want his people to go after grants. He didn't need [this money]." At the time Peruggi was appointed president, external funding was not considered necessary.

Resolution

Peruggi confronted these significant challenges as she set out to improve student success, improve graduation rates, address remedial education, and raise funds. Her commitment to the community college mission was a guide: "I'd seen what community colleges did when I was in continuing education. I saw how much they did. They're such an important piece of what makes this city better because the community college students are the people who stay here, and they are the people that are running this city. They're your nurses, people in the health services, people who work in the police force. They really are the backbone of the city."

Peruggi was not one to be daunted by challenges. While perceiving her marginalization at the central leadership level in the CUNY system, she recognized and used the autonomy that was afforded her as president of KCC. She believed deeply in the power of leadership to create change, particularly through an approach that "was supportive, down to earth, and focused." Peruggi was very much a relationship-based leader. She demonstrated this trait through the innovative use of task forces and feedback to departments combined with a highly personal approach (such as handwritten birthday cards to all staff). The foundational goal for institutional change was to instill trust in her and the institution—which she saw as the essential building block for her presidency.

Peruggi's leadership involved empowerment she hoped would usher in a new spirit at the college. She provided support and a failsafe atmosphere she felt were essential for innovation; even more, she made changes that she identified as necessary, if not urgent. Describing her leadership style, she spoke in terms of *we* rather than *I*, a parsing of language that revealed her dedication to collaboration and teamwork. Even more, Peruggi identified her job as president as establishing structures that empowered and enabled employees to strive to enhance student success.

Peruggi recognizes that a new spirit of empowerment requires a rejuvenated and innovative culture: "We focused on the individuals that work there. I see my job as a president to create an environment where people can do their best work, where they want to do good stuff. . . . My major responsibility is to create that kind of environment so that people feel good about their work—they feel dignified, they want to work hard, they feel like they are moving forward, and [they are] focused on students."

Asked whether her caring, listening attitude was a factor in her success, Peruggi observes, "I think it was. And being in touch with people. Faculty knew that every semester, I would come to their department for a meeting. . . . I would come every year to their department at least once if not twice and talk with them and listen to them and hear their complaints. I think that was really important. They felt that I wasn't so distant from them."

Peruggi was also clear that while she set the priorities and calls to action, she wanted to create a space for employees to take ownership. Peruggi encouraged employees to not fear failure. She wants faculty and staff to "figure out what we're going to do, agree on it, then go do it and tell me about it. Keep in touch about how it's going. Figure out if it's going haywire, how to correct it. I liked to try a lot of things. Let's do something. I have more of a style of 'Let's do it,' and if it doesn't work out, OK. Things have to move. If we just sit, we're going to go backward."

In approaching this culture change, Peruggi drew on a lesson from a German psychologist at her first job as a drug-abuse counselor in a state jail in the 1970s: "Every parole officer, every social worker came from miles around to see this man. . . . One parole officer . . . raised his hand and said, 'Is there anything that we shouldn't do? Is there something that's really forbidden? That would be the worst thing that we could for our clients?' [The psychologist] said, 'Don't put poison in their soup.' I never forgot that. And I thought [about KCC], we can do anything. . . . We've got to change. We can try almost anything. Nobody is going to be pointed at."

To gain trust, Peruggi knew she had to listen. She laid the groundwork by meeting with everyone who worked at the college. She invited groups of twenty-five people to her office for coffee. Groups were mixed: grounds staff with enrollment management professionals and faculty and so on. It took over a year. Looking back, Peruggi remarks, "Some of those people had been at that school for twenty-five years and had never been in the president's office. The first group came in, and they were terrified. They thought I was going to fire them. I said, 'Don't be ridiculous. Come on in.'" From that experience, Peruggi was able to isolate the value shared by everyone at KCC: "It's like a family. So that gives you a clue how to proceed."

She also asked employees to identify the one thing they would change. All identified the registration system. Peruggi immediately assessed that if she could improve this system, then, in her words, "it would validate the fact that I listened and give me a win. That I had the power to change things and that I would change things."

Peruggi did not proceed alone or take a top-down approach. Rather than convene a team of senior administrators, she assembled a task force of students, staff, faculty, and what she called "live wires" from around the college. Their charge was this: change the registration system by next semester. Peruggi told the group, "I don't know how to do it. But you are going to have to figure it out. It's going to change." She says, "And we did. We changed it a little by the first semester. And then the next fall, we put it online."

To tackle planning for remediation courses, Peruggi applied the same approach. She established an enrollment management committee, also comprised of a mix of students, faculty, and staff. Her mandate, despite the resistance of the staff, was that every student would be required to take English plus additional remediation classes. The new enrollment management committee was tasked with the execution and planning: "They had never brought people from different departments together, such as faculty members, student affairs, admissions. They began to learn how to work together and look at admissions and who's coming in and what were they testing at and what classes we would need so we'd have enough. They'd never done that before in any systematic way. That really got people working together in a different way."

At the same time, she instituted a new practice where she would meet with departments every year to talk about their annual reviews. According to Peruggi, department chairs and faculty appreciate the opportunity to contextualize the standardized departmental reviews required by CUNY. Although Peruggi did not shy away from discussing areas that needed improvement, she set out to seek faculty input on strategies for improvement. This also allowed Peruggi to introduce her collaborative approach early in her tenure, and this was a practice she continued throughout her time at CUNY.

Peruggi applied the same relationship-based approach to fundraising and board development. She tapped friends and colleagues across the city. She revived and altered the composition of the board, replacing them with significant members of her network, calling on her own friends—even colleagues and board members from Marymount Manhattan College. She connected with businesses and other leaders in Brooklyn, where KCC is located, linking them to the college's mission. She asked for recommendations for board members, then tapped local stakeholders. Each board member was asked to give $1,000. Peruggi raised a scholarship for a student from one of her contacts in the Brooklyn area.

At the same time, she launched a new initiative to engage alumni. Although the early events were mostly attended by her friends, Peruggi began to build a sense of community and attachment by establishing homecoming as an annual celebration; throwing parties on the beach that included not only alumni but also donors, friends, and prospective friends and supporters; and eventually organizing a benefit to raise funds.

Peruggi had a big and ambitious vision. She accomplished a great deal through decisive decision-making and creating an empowering and supporting culture. Although she effectively used the hands-off approach of CUNY leadership over Kingsborough, she reached outside the university to generate the perception that KCC was on the move. As she reports,

> We went from nowhere in terms of CUNY. [We weren't] the worst school but the school they [CUNY leadership] never paid attention to because we were out there at the beach, and we were doing fine and never gave them any trouble. We never gave them anything to be excited about. The budget was always managed. . . . There started to be a buzz. We started to get more students. Things started to feel good. . . . We were lucky in a lot of stuff. When [President] Obama was elected, we got Jill Biden to come and give the commencement speech. And I saw that as a tremendous coup.

Peruggi put advertisements for KCC in movie theaters, got funding for a shuttle bus from the subway station to KCC to shorten commutes, and looked outside the university for recognition.

Perhaps the best-known initiative that Peruggi expanded was the college's Learning Community Program. The program was started for students for whom English was a foreign language. The vision was to create cohesive student communities and higher pass rates using a course-cluster concept. Groups of up to twenty-five first-year students were gathered together and were required to take a three-semester cluster: English (usually at the remedial level), a course on another academic subject, and a one-credit freshman orientation course. The three instructors in the learning community collaborated on integrating the courses, meeting regularly to review individual students' progress and strategizing on barriers to students' retention. Resources included tutoring, book vouchers, counselors, and extra mentoring. Using an experimental design in its initial phases, students were randomly assigned to the learning communities and compared to those taking the regular course schedule. Early reports showed that although the communities did not improve retention, participants had higher course pass rates and were more likely to pass their remedial requirements.

Peruggi scaled up the program so that by 2010, 80 percent of Kingsborough students were participating in the program, and retention rates improved. Under her leadership, Kingsborough gained national recognition for the successful outcomes associated with its use of learning communities. In June 2005, encouraged by early findings from participation in Manpower Demonstration Research Corporation's Opening Doors Demonstration project, Kingsborough scaled up its learning community program to serve most incoming freshman. Over a six-year period, student retention rates increased from 64 percent to 70 percent. The graduation rate increased from 25 percent to 35 percent—eight points higher than any other community college in the CUNY system and among the highest in the nation for community colleges.[9] In 2006, KCC won a $100,000 grant from the Ford Foundation to replicate its successful learning communities nationwide, signaling the educational leadership of the institution.

KCC continued to undergo an upward trajectory in terms of national visibility and student success. More external accolades followed. According to a profile in the *Forum for Youth Investment* in 2011, "[Dr. Peruggi's] leadership fostered the redesign of whole divisions and the creation of new services. Classroom practices shifted. The college revamped admissions and advising, and centralized enrollment services—moves that changed institutional culture and integrated disparate best practices into a more cohesive whole. The entire institution became focused on student success, and no part remained unchanged."[10]

In Peruggi's penultimate year as president, Kingsborough Community College was one of four community colleges selected as a Finalist with Distinction in the Aspen Institute College Excellence Program. As a top-four college, KCC was awarded a $1 million prize, recognizing achievement in four primary areas: student learning outcomes, degree and college completion, labor market success in students securing jobs after college, and minority and low-income student success.[11]

At the time of the award, KCC was outperforming other colleges in student graduation and transfer rates as well as the career prospects enjoyed by its graduates. According to the press release distributed at the time of the award, the college's statistics speak for themselves:

- Sixty percent of students transferred to four-year colleges, compared with the national average of 26 percent.
- Five years after completing their degrees, graduates earn about $41,000—comparable to the wages of all other workers in the area.[12]

Josh Wyner, executive director of the Aspen Institute College Excellence Program, describes KCC's success in these terms: "Kingsborough Community College has achieved strong results in graduation, transfer, and employment outcomes while working with an extremely diverse group of students, many who face challenging life circumstances. . . . Its staff and faculty are deeply committed to removing the roadblocks that keep so many community college students from finishing what they start."[13] Kingsborough's accomplishments were recognized outside of education circles as well, with features in the *New York Times*, the *Daily News*, CBS television, and local media outlets.

Clearly, the signal change in Peruggi's vision required a shift in institutional culture. Peruggi's focus was always on creating the institutional and infrastructure systems that promoted student success. Her relationship-oriented leadership style created the conditions for these achievements, along with having her ear to the ground, empowering faculty and staff, and engendering pride and innovation. By this account, she successfully executed what she considers her core principle as president of KCC: "Creating an environment where people can do their best work."

Notes

1   "Women Shaping History 2011: President Regina Peruggi, Kingsborough Community College," *Education Update Online*, March–April 2011, http://www.educationupdate.com/archives/2011/MAR/html/cov-ReginaPeruggi.html.

2   Mary Visher and Jedediah Teres, *Breaking New Ground: An Impact Study of Career-Focused Learning Communities at Kingsborough Community College* (New York: National Center for Postsecondary Research, 2011), 13.

3   Regina Peruggi, in discussion with the author, July 6, 2018. All direct quotes are taken from this interview unless otherwise noted.

4   Visher and Teres, *Breaking New Ground*, 9.

5   Ibid., 13.

6   Ibid., 1.

7   Ibid., 2.

8   Ibid., 13.

9   Alicia Wilson-Ahlstrom and Nicole Yohalem, *Changing the Odds for Students: Spotlight on Kingsborough College* (Washington, D.C.: Ready by 21, 2011).

10 Ibid.

11 "Kingsborough Community College (CUNY) Named One of Top Four Community Colleges in America," Achieving the Dream, March 19, 2013, https://www.achievingthedream.org/news/6727/kingsborough-community-college-cuny-named-one-of-top-four-community-colleges-in-america-by-aspen-institute.

12 Ibid.

13 Ibid.

The Reinventor

Pat McGuire and the Transformation of Trinity Washington University

Elizabeth Kiss

Background

As she approaches three decades at the helm of Trinity Washington University, President Pat McGuire is not slowing down. Her knees may trouble her when she walks, but she remains a woman on a mission and in a hurry. She speaks with fierce and frank intelligence, leaning forward to make a point just as she does with such effectiveness in her frequent appearances to give testimony on Capitol Hill about issues in higher education. Her eyes gleam with pride as she talks about Trinity Washington's latest triumphs—such as its $1 million Inclusive Excellence grant for the teaching of science from Howard Hughes Medical Institute[1]—and with anger as she decries the attacks by President Trump on DREAMers, undocumented students striving for legal status and American citizenship.

In recent years, McGuire has received an extraordinary litany of honors, including major higher education awards such as the 2016 Hesburgh Award for Leadership Excellence from the Teacher Insurance and Annuity Association (TIAA) Institute, the 2015 Carnegie Award for Academic Leadership from the Carnegie Corporation, and the 2012 Henry Paley Award from the National Association of Independent Colleges and Universities.[2] Her fellow Catholics have recognized her with the 2018 Presidents' Distinguished Service Award from the Association of Catholic Colleges and Universities and the 2017 Robert M. Holstein Faith Doing Justice Award from the Ignatian Solidarity Network.[3] She was named Leader of the Year in 2007 by the Greater Washington Board of Trade and has appeared on every annual list of Washington's most powerful women.[4] And her courageous commentary on public issues earned her the 2010 Alexander Meiklejohn Award for Academic Freedom from the American Association of University Professors.[5]

Not bad for someone who describes herself as an accidental president, who took on the role in 1989 at the age of thirty-six at a time when Trinity was beset by plummeting enrollment, desperate finances, and accreditation challenges. As McGuire recalls the occasion, "fix it or close it" was the task given to her by the board.[6]

McGuire did indeed fix Trinity—by reinventing it. Her presidency is a story of institutional adaptation to changing times as she took a proud but dying elite, predominantly white, Catholic women's college and turned it into a diverse powerhouse of urban higher education. Her success reflects her ability to combine fierce devotion to Trinity's core mission with a courageous willingness to adapt that mission to new circumstances.

Her long tenure has required McGuire to tackle a series of successive challenges: a broken business model, accreditation issues, backlash from angry traditionalist alumnae, explosive racial divisions on campus, the Great Recession, the Trump presidency, and more. Through grit and entrepreneurial spirit, she has established herself within what is still a male-dominated DC educational and business establishment. And in the tradition of radical Catholic educators, she has stood up for what she believes, becoming one of the most outspoken higher education leaders of our time.

Great college presidents find ways to balance continuity and change, crafting an institutional narrative that combines fidelity to the mission with a clear mandate for innovation. When institutions face existential crises requiring more radical changes, this balance is especially difficult to strike. The leader ultimately has to persuade institutional stakeholders to let go of some of their cherished notions of "who we are, always have been, always will be" while retaining their sense of connection and allegiance.

McGuire's reinvention of Trinity is exceptional. She persuaded the college's stakeholders to move past a particular image of Trinity—

white, highly selective, majority Catholic—by invoking an older story of what Trinity stood for: opening doors of opportunity to women who would otherwise be overlooked and left behind.

So while McGuire led a pivotal shift in Trinity's identity, her presidency has built on the legacy of earlier leaders of the college who shared her commitment to educating and empowering women. To understand that continuity, we have to look at the history of Trinity's founding order, the Sisters of Notre Dame de Namur.

Trinity College was established in 1897 by the Sisters of Notre Dame de Namur, a religious order dedicated to the education of girls and women and marked by a willingness to confront traditional authorities within and beyond the church.

As Kevin Carey explains in an engaging profile of Trinity in *Washington Monthly*, every Catholic religious order has a charism—a distinctive mission, ethos, and temperament. The charism of the Sisters of Notre Dame de Namur centers on running schools for women and girls but also "a spirit of ambitious enterprise and fierce autonomy—a refusal to take no for an answer in the face of institutional authority."[7]

The order was founded in 1804 in France by two women, a shop owner's daughter named Julie Billiart and Viscountess Francoise Blin de Bourdon. As loyal Catholics in revolutionary anticlerical times, Billiart and de Bourdon faced threats of mob violence and execution. With de Bourdon's support, Billiart was able to establish convents and schools for girls. But her egalitarian ideas soon clashed with the local Catholic authorities, and in 1809, an angry bishop forced Billiart and her fledgling order into exile in Namur, Belgium, where the order's motherhouse remains today.[8]

"Most people think of nuns as little shy retiring people," McGuire notes. "They're not. They were revolutionaries."[9] Within a few decades, the sisters had crossed the Atlantic and established a network of girls' schools nationwide. By the end of the nineteenth century, the sisters felt called to take the next step and provide Catholic women with access to higher education. But to achieve this goal, they had to win what some commentators dubbed "the War of 1897."[10]

In March 1897, two of the order's leaders, Sister Susan McGroarty and Sister Mary Euphrasia, met with the vice-rector of the recently established Catholic University, James Garrigan. Twenty women had recently applied and been refused admission by the all-male institution. Garrigan shared the sisters' concern that excluding women from Catholic higher education would force them to attend Protestant or infidel institutions. And so McGroarty, Euphrasia, and Garrigan joined forces to establish Trinity College for Women.[11]

The project was soon engulfed in controversy. One Catholic University professor, Joseph Schroeder, reached out to Vatican allies to try to scuttle it. "The project of a university for the weaker sex," noted a missive from Rome, "has made a disagreeable impression here."[12] Conservative Catholic newspapers decried the "new-fangled rise of the New Woman." But the sisters were not deterred. They promoted their vision with tireless energy and determination and ultimately secured support from the archbishop. Trinity College enrolled its first students in November 1900.

In establishing Trinity, the sisters weren't only interested in giving young Catholic women the chance to go to a college that upheld Catholic values. They wanted to create an institution for Catholic women that would "do for them what Vassar and Wellesley and Bryn Mawr [were] doing for American women." Trinity would be a peer institution of the northeastern women's colleges known as the Seven Sisters. The curriculum was modeled on the Seven Sisters, and incoming students "were expected to demonstrate proficiency in Latin, English, either French or German, history, and mathematics."[13]

Over the next few decades, Trinity became a college of choice for Catholic women across the country.[14] Many of the early graduates went into the sisterhood or teaching, but some became trailblazers in medicine, business, law, and social work. Jane Hoey (class of 1914) headed up the Welfare Council of New York City and was appointed by President Roosevelt to direct the Bureau of Public Assistance, becoming one of the most powerful women in the federal government.

In 1959, Trinity appointed Sister Margaret Claydon (class of 1945), then only thirty-six years old, as president. In her opening press conference, she told *Time*, "Educated women must have definite views and standards. They must know the good from the bad and be able to say why." She added, "The modern world needs more people—including girls—who think for themselves." Claydon thought that education for women should be stiffened and that more women should go on to graduate school and be fitted for "a better contribution to American life." About Trinity, she added, "We're not in the business of training committee women or bridge players."[15]

Claydon, who served as president until 1975 and remains, at the age of ninety-five, an ardent champion of Trinity, became a major architect of Trinity's educational ethos. Reflecting back decades later on her approach to students, she notes, "We treated them like *women*, not like little girls." She wanted Trinity students to be strong and self-reliant. Students were encouraged to think about their broader social responsibilities and to pursue professional ambitions. By 1965, fifty-seven Trinity alumnae had earned medical degrees. Seniors were encouraged to take the Graduate Record Examinations (GRE), and of the roughly 3,400 women who graduated from Trinity between 1955 and 1975, more than half went on to earn advanced degrees.[16]

The school attracted students like Nancy Pelosi, daughter of the mayor of Baltimore, and Kathleen Sebelius, daughter of the governor of Ohio.[17] Pelosi (class of 1962) became the first female Speaker of the House in U.S. history, and Sebelius (class of 1970), served as governor of Kansas and secretary of health and human services. Pelosi and Sebelius collaborated to gain passage of the Affordable Care Act in 2011 and had their picture taken with President Obama, explaining they were Trinity sisters.[18]

Other prominent Trinity alumnae from this era include the eight-term Connecticut congresswoman Barbara Kennelly (class of 1958), *USA Today* and Hearst Magazines president Cathie Black (class of 1966), Pulitzer Prize winner Caryle Murphy (class of 1968), U.S. district court judge Claire Eagan (class of 1972), ambassador for nuclear nonproliferation Susan Burk (class of 1976), and chief of staff to first lady Hillary Clinton, Maggie Williams (class of 1977). The cumulative public impact of Trinity women is remarkable.

As Sister Claydon's bracing words to *Time* demonstrate, Trinity was not only a college of choice for middle- and upper-class Catholic women but had a radical bent. A 1965 speech Claydon gave to the National Catholic Education Association captures her commitment to education as emancipation. "If we are really seeking through education to nurture international understanding," Claydon argued, "we have to be willing to abandon the merely acceptable views and to acquaint our students with controversy and problematic knowledge." She went on, "Rather than holding up submission and conformity as standards to meet, we have to encourage our students of today to take stands that may be unpopular, that may even expose them to ostracism, debate, controversy, initiative—these must be the hallmarks of educated people today. We are in a *learning* society. Our students must be characterized as those prepared to go on learning."[19]

It is no surprise, then, that when the civil rights and antiwar movements surged in the 1960s, Trinity students—and many of the nuns—got involved. The dean of students kept a cash reserve on hand to bail protesters out of jail.[20]

It was into this heady mixture of academic rigor and political ferment that Pat McGuire arrived in 1970, wearing skirts and knee socks, a first-generation student on a full scholarship. A conservative kid from a Nixon household, she was one of seven siblings in an Irish Italian Philadelphia family. Coming to Trinity changed her life.[21]

Within months, she had dived into political activism. "To come away to Washington to go to college was so exciting," she told Michel Martin at National Public Radio in 2010. "It was a wonderful place to be. . . . We were very much engaged with politics in Washington at that time. Those were the days of the anti-war movement, the student mobilization. So we spent a lot of time doing that kind of activity. . . . It was great fun."[22]

She majored in political science, played basketball, and graduated from Trinity *cum laude*. After graduation, she entered Georgetown University Law School and then, finding legal practice boring, became director of the school's Street Law Clinic. When funding dried up for that program, she became director of development and eventually assistant dean at Georgetown Law and led a $15 million campaign to build the Edward Bennett Williams Law Library.

Following in the footsteps of so many of her Trinity sisters, McGuire stepped into the public arena, serving as a legal commentator on the CBS educational program 30 *Minutes* and on *Panorama* for local television channel WTTB-TV.[23] By her midthirties, she was a lawyer, a midlevel university administrator, and a television commentator. She joined the Trinity College alumnae association and became its president.

While McGuire's career had blossomed, her alma mater had fallen on hard times. By 1989, the *Washington Post* was writing that Trinity had collapsed. McGuire penned a letter to the editor challenging this prognosis. Recalling the 1948 Chicago newspaper headline that had prematurely declared President Truman's electoral defeat, she wrote, "Harry Truman went on to win. So will we."[24]

Trinity College had indeed fallen on hard times, with full-time enrollment falling from one thousand in 1969 to three hundred in 1989.[25] Several factors combined to produce this crisis. First, as all-male colleges started admitting women, women's colleges experienced a rapid migration of their best applicants to these former bastions of male privilege. Sister Margaret Claydon recalls the president of Georgetown University telling her smugly, a few years after his school went co-ed, "We're getting the young women Trinity used to get."[26]

Then as more professional opportunities opened up for Catholic women, fewer went into the sisterhood. And as McGuire explains, Vatican II "changed the financial basis of the institutions. The nuns worked for free in these institutions, and then after the Second Vatican Council . . . the sisters left and went on to other ministries. So financially, we lost our free labor."[27]

Scores of women's colleges went co-ed or bankrupt or merged with their male counterparts. At Trinity, steep enrollment declines led to leadership turmoil and ideological arguments between those committed to sustaining Trinity's elite status and others who, as McGuire recalled, "didn't think it was missional to educate privileged white women" and argued it would be better to close and sell the property.

The college's twelfth president, Sister Donna Jurick, devised a creative idea to stabilize the budget in the early 1980s. She opened a weekend college for working women, drawing a racially diverse population from the city that had previously been ignored by the college. The program, the first of its kind in Washington, was wildly popular and within three years had eclipsed the undergraduate program in enrollment.[28]

But Jurick's solution provoked furious dissent among students and alumnae who saw it as a betrayal of the school's liberal arts tradition. It also raised the ire of faculty whose workloads had increased without much consultation. Jurick was forced out in 1987. The school then hired James J. McGrath, an experienced college president, as the first man and layperson to run Trinity. But he failed to calm the troubled waters and left after just eighteen months.

It was then that the trustees turned to alumnae association president McGuire, telling her, "Fix it or close it." Like Sister Margaret Claydon when she assumed the presidency thirty years earlier, McGuire was only thirty-six years old. But the circumstances she confronted were wildly different.

"I was the sixth person in eight years in the president's office," McGuire recalled. It sounded to her like "a good job for a kid with a short attention span."

Resolution

The challenges facing McGuire were daunting: declining enrollment, a budget deficit, tough questions from accreditors about the school's finances, a demoralized faculty, and alumnae who were devoted to the college but wedded to an unrealistic hope that the students who had fled—white, middle-class, suburban Catholic women—could be lured back.

"We had an incoming class of seventy students," McGuire recalls. "And then the next year, it was sixty. At one point the District of Columbia actually thought we had closed." At her first faculty meeting, she was greeted "with dead silence."

Drawing on what she calls her skills as a lawyer, advocate, and talker, McGuire began asking big questions. She asked for trend data and was told, "Trinity is *not* trendy." So she started sharing trend and cost analyses with the faculty. Pointing out that forty-two faculty could not sustain fifty majors, she told the faculty, "Financially, we can't support more than fifteen majors. Tell me where to spend the funds." She worked steadily to clean up the finances and prepared to launch a fundraising campaign.

In her strategic planning discussions with trustees, McGuire raised core questions about Trinity's mission. "If we wanted to try to educate one thousand white Irish Catholics, we would have to go co-ed," she said, though it would have been difficult to attain this goal with two large Catholic co-educational institutions nearby, Georgetown and Catholic University. But even if it had been possible, she said, "where was our historic mission to serve women?"

If the school remained committed to educating women, it needed to attract a different population of them. Looking at the enrollment figures, McGuire wondered, "How many students do we have from Washington, DC, public schools?" and was told, "None. They can't do the work here."

But McGuire emphasizes that it was the nuns who drove the key conversation as trustees began to consider the idea of refocusing Trinity on serving a more racially diverse population of students from Washington. Indeed, throughout the turbulent early years of her presidency, she felt blessed to have the support of the Sisters of Notre Dame de Namur. "They said to me . . . 'Stop trying so hard to reclaim the old population. There are hundreds of thousands on our doorstep here in Washington who need this kind of education.' And they were right."[29]

As she reflects on her long tenure, McGuire distinguishes between three chapters, dubbing the 1990s "her first presidency" and acknowledging that it was a treacherous, tumultuous, stressful time. Just as she was starting to make headway in reformulating Trinity's mission and stabilizing the college, with enrollment rising and the college's modest endowment growing to $5 million, McGuire was hit with the first of three crises: a campaign by a group of alumnae to oust her.

The Alumnae Action Committee began collecting negative stories about McGuire and called for her resignation, sending a scathing letter to all alumnae claiming that McGuire was destroying the college's liberal arts and Catholic traditions. Some also expressed discontent over the shifting racial demographics of the campus as Trinity enrolled more black students. In a *Washington Post* account at the time, one alumna lamented that the school was "adapting to contemporary society."[30] It was an extraordinarily painful episode for McGuire as a former alumnae association president. But the issue was officially resolved when the board ousted the critics for breaching their fiduciary duties, revoked the alumnae association's right to elect board members, and placed its budget under the control of the college administration. An ally of McGuire and the board, Peggy O'Brien (class of 1969), then won a landslide election as a write-in candidate for the alumnae association presidency. O'Brien took on the difficult task of rebuilding confidence in the college and its leadership. "She rode the alumnae circuit for three years," McGuire explains admiringly. O'Brien ultimately became chair of the board, one of a series of strong board chairs who have partnered with McGuire over the years.

The next big challenge was getting Trinity through its reaccreditation process from the Middle States Commission on Higher Education. The accreditor had had the college on a watch list since the 1950s for financial reasons, McGuire explains. The reason was simple: "Trinity had no money." But when financial challenges were coupled with low enrollment, restive alumnae, and accreditors committed to exercising tough love, the process was daunting. A group of disgruntled alumnae tried to meet with accreditors to air their grievances. But ultimately, McGuire said, after the visiting team reviewed the campus self-study and strategic plan and spoke to McGuire and others about their vision and plans for Trinity, they issued a glowing and affirming report.

Finally, in 1996, the campus was rocked by an anonymous eight-page hate letter left in mailboxes attacking blacks, lesbians, and other minorities. It purported to be from the White Student Alliance. Although its author was never identified, it broke open fault lines around race relations on campus as African American students demanded greater recognition and complained of insensitivity to their needs.[31] The story hit the media, and McGuire found herself in the middle of a racial crisis.

McGuire reflected on this episode in a 2015 editorial written after University of Missouri system president Tim Wolfe was forced to resign following months of student protests over his administration's handling of racist incidents at Mizzou. "We had forums—oh, my goodness, we had forums!" she wrote. "We had faculty meetings, late nights in dorms and raucous debates about free speech (was 'the letter' an exercise in free speech?) and racism (is racism only one way? were some black students being racist toward white students? why were the Latina students feeling left out?)."[32]

The experience of being "in the crucible of racial anger on campus" taught her valuable lessons about leadership. The first was humility, learning "to sit in the middle of crowded rooms overheated with emotion and allow the waves of anger to keep breaking overhead," to "admit that I could never fully know what my students felt."[33] She also had to stand up and lead despite her fears: "I was deeply afraid of saying the wrong thing . . . [and] truly afraid that we would lose Trinity itself, a precarious institution in those days that had almost no margin for error. I learned that the only way to fight the fire is to walk right through it. Learning to speak out loud about prejudice and fear, racial mythologies and the real facts about institutional racism became essential to moving forward."[34]

Finally, it was critical for her to take concrete steps to make Trinity a more inclusive institution. In the end, McGuire's hardest conversations were not with the black students but with the faculty as she sought specific commitments to diversify curricula and faculty hiring. Some professors pushed back, citing academic freedom. But she held firm, launching Trinity on a process that would result, two decades later, in a faculty that is more than 50 percent African American, Latina, and Asian.[35]

Thanks to McGuire's courageous leadership, the crisis precipitated by the White Student Alliance letter proved to be a positive turning point for Trinity. "We learned to talk about race," she explains. "It was liberating." And so, McGuire told me, as it celebrated its centenary on Founder's Day, August 20, 1997, complete with a procession of horses, buggies, and nuns down North Capitol Street, Trinity College "claimed [its] place and space in the city" and embraced a new identity "as a predominantly black institution serving a distinctive population of low-income students from the Washington region."[36]

By the end of her first decade, McGuire had survived crises that would have derailed most college presidents. She had secured the financial viability of Trinity as a women's college through a paradigm shift in the population of women it served. The demographic changes were dramatic: from 1989 to 2000, the student body changed from more than 85 percent white to more than 60 percent black, from predominantly Catholic to predominantly Baptist and other Christian denominations, and from middle class to low income.[37] And while the full-time undergraduate population remained small, a growing number of students attended Trinity's evening, weekend, and part-time programs for adults.

But as McGuire related to me, many of the same structural tensions that had plagued Sister Donna Jurick's presidency remained, with a struggle for primacy between different parts of the institution: full and part time, traditional and adult, liberal arts and professional education. McGuire's next challenge was to integrate Trinity and make it greater than the sum of its parts.

McGuire's second decade as president saw dramatic growth and change at Trinity, most visibly with the decision in 2004 to become Trinity Washington University. The name change signified a recognition that "diversification is a permanent part of our future," McGuire explains. Gone was the notion that the part-time programs for adults were a temporary measure to subsidize the college's core full-time program. Instead, Trinity embraced a broader mission as a comprehensive university preparing students across the lifespan. A new structure gave each unit its own dean. The historic full-time undergraduate women's college became the College of Arts and Sciences, while Trinity's graduate programs in education became a School of Education and Sister Donna Jurick's weekend program evolved into the School of Professional Studies. In 2007, the School of Nursing and Health Professions was added. Although the College of Arts and Sciences remained a women's college, all the other schools were co-ed.

Trinity's new mission statement affirmed "commitment to the education of women" as the first of four core values, noting that this commitment was carried out both through the design and pedagogy of the "historic undergraduate women's college" and "by advancing principles of equity, justice, and honor in the education of women and men in all other programs."[38]

This broadening of Trinity's structure and mission was accompanied by what McGuire has described as "profound change—a true paradigm shift—in curricula and programs, services and support systems, policies and practices, and in the size and capacity of faculty and staff to work successfully with a new student population." Instead of "focusing on our students as unprepared for us," she adds, Trinity had to come to "an understanding that we had to be better prepared for them."[39]

These changes required strong faculty leadership. McGuire deployed faculty retreats as a tool for planning and buy-in and provided retirement incentives to encourage those older faculty who were unable or unwilling to embrace the changes to make room for a new generation of professors.

It is a measure of McGuire's success in shifting attitudes that the name change to Trinity Washington University was enthusiastically embraced by alumnae. The Middle States Accreditation visiting team in 2006 commented in its report on "the breath-taking achievement" at Trinity, noting "above all . . . the success of Trinity faculty in curricular and pedagogical change serving the students of the paradigm shift." The accreditation team also noted "the impressive congruence" between Trinity in 2006 and the original vision of Trinity's founders in 1897, adding, "The team admires and commends the University's rejection of the notion that paradigm shift means abandonment of historic mission. Rather, we discover in the work and vitality of Trinity of 2006, a most obvious continuity with Trinity's 110 year old mission expressed with a renewed relevance and vigor."[40]

These changes led to an impressive enrollment surge, with over two thousand students enrolled across all Trinity's programs by 2010.[41] McGuire told me she was also able to raise funds to build the first new building on Trinity's campus in decades, the Trinity Center for Women and Girls in Sports, a $20 million, 62,000-square-foot facility that offers provisions for the campus and the neighborhood and gets forty thousand visitors a year.

Trinity embraced partnerships and entrepreneurial activities, hosting Elderhostel and welcoming four thousand teachers per year for professional development programs.[42] As part of its commitment to the long-neglected Washington neighborhoods east of the Anacostia River, it became the educational partner to an innovative humanitarian campus on the east side, THEARC, offering college classes to adults from these impoverished neighborhoods.[43]

All this activity and growth made the university and its entrepreneurial president more visible in the Washington community. McGuire joined the board of Washington Hospital Center and was named 2007 Leader of the Year by the Greater Washington Board of Trade.

A 2010 profile in the *Washington Post* praised McGuire's extraordinary energy and commitment, describing her as "the smiling face of Trinity at nearly every game, performance, or campus event. She gives out the freshman medals at orientation; she hands seniors their diplomas at graduation. To many of these students, Pat McGuire *is* Trinity." A freshman basketball player told the *Post*, "She's out there hooting your name, chest-bumping, giving you a high-five. . . . Stuff like that makes you feel like you're cared about."[44]

There were potholes along the way, of course. The nursing school got off to a difficult start and had to suspend its adult programs to maintain academic quality. Fundraising for a new academic center ground to a halt in the wake of the Great Recession. And Trinity's sports teams, McGuire admits ruefully, "are still generally terrible." But Trinity has sustained the momentum established in the 2000s. Today, it enrolls 2,300 students. And thanks to a $10 million lead gift from Jean Payden (class of 1953) and a successful fundraising campaign, McGuire ultimately succeeded in 2016 in opening the first new academic building on campus in fifty years, the $32 million Payden Academic Center, a game changer for the teaching of science and nursing at Trinity.[45]

In her third decade as president, McGuire is intensely focused on putting Trinity at the cutting edge of higher education. She is excited about the creative efforts in science pedagogy led by Trinity faculty, including three Clare Booth Luce professors, and by the innovative developments made possible by what she calls the booster shot of Trinity's $1 million Inclusive Excellence grant from the Howard Hughes Medical Institute. She wants Trinity to be a national leader in inspiring low-income women to become scientists, offering them undergraduate research opportunities that blend training in traditional scientific skills with art, poetry, and song. She is encouraging Trinity faculty to rethink majors and create interdisciplinary clusters in areas like the social sciences. And as for the frequently posed question about her timetable for retirement, while emphasizing that she serves at the pleasure of her board, she says bluntly, "I'm not done."

But the most distinctive element of the third chapter of McGuire's presidency is her emergence as a thought leader and one of the most outspoken educators of our time. She has testified before Congress on college costs and student loan reform, spoken to education groups about institutional transformation; written op-eds, blogs, and *Huffington Post* and *Washington Post* columns; and used her Twitter account, @TrinityPrez, to speak up on a wide range of issues, from Catholic church sex-abuse scandals to issues of race and immigration.

Incisive and plainspoken, she called the Obama administration's proposed regulations on teacher education "Orwellian"[46] and criticized the "religious vigilantism" of fellow Catholics who tried to disrupt President Obama's speech at Notre Dame.[47] She recommended that the bishop of Washington resign.[48] She has become a vocal critic of the Trump administration's anti-immigration policies and attacks on the media and even wrote a blog post condemning a high-profile Trinity alumna and donor:

> Presidential Counselor Kellyanne Conway, Trinity class of 1989, has played a large role in facilitating the manipulation of facts and encouraging the grave injustice being perpetrated by the Trump

administration's war on immigrants among many other issues. . . .
Some people admire her staunch advocacy for her client's positions,
and others applaud the fact that she was the first woman to manage
a successful presidential campaign. But in fact . . . her advocacy on
his behalf is often at variance with the truth. Ms. Conway invented
the now-infamous phrase "alternative facts" to defend Trump's
claims about the size of crowds at his inauguration [and] has been
part of a team that thinks nothing of shaping and spreading a skein
of lies as a means to secure power.[49]

When many commentators, including an angry Conway, con-
demned McGuire's statements as politically partisan, McGuire was
unrepentant: "If we academics don't stand for truth, what's the purpose of what we do?"[50]

McGuire's willingness to speak out on topics other college presidents will not touch is deeply grounded in her core mission as an
educator. In her speech accepting the 2010 Alexander Meiklejohn
Award for Academic Freedom, she forcefully laid out her convictions: "Higher education is one of the great counterbalances to
government in a free society, but that balance only works through
the free and frequent exercise of the muscle of our mission. . . .
Our stewardship . . . requires us to swing mighty axes against the
restraints that compromise our ability to conduct research freely,
publish whatever we choose, teach as we must, and speak openly
without fear."[51]

Describing the threats to academic freedom from government,
the church, and above all, from "the tendency to self-censorship,"
she encouraged her peers to speak out: "Academic freedom rarely
dies in one egregious event . . . [it] erodes in a thousand small
concessions. . . . We presidents can either cower under our desks . . .
or we can do our jobs, with responsibility, with integrity, with
audacity."[52]

In each decade at the helm of Trinity, McGuire has widened her
circle of influence. She first transformed her own campus, then
turned it into a significant player in Washington's educational landscape and a successful model for educating a diverse, low-income

student population. And by asserting higher education's moral responsibility to defend the principles of a free society, she has taken on a thought leadership role of national significance.

As McGuire had predicted in her 1989 letter to the *Washington Post*, Trinity, like Truman, went on to win, in large measure because of her leadership. Asked to identify larger leadership lessons from her experience, McGuire says, "If you want to create change, tell the truth. And don't get scared by the noise."

Her commitment to telling the truth, so critical to her ability to convince the Trinity community of the necessity for change, is also evident in the tough love she dispenses to her women's college colleagues. She rejects the dominant narrative that women's colleges must decide between staying single-sex or going coed, arguing that this way of framing the issue is a "sixties solution for a twentieth-century industry." Instead, she urges women's colleges to imagine relevant, economically sustainable institutional models—based on their institution's specific assets—that include women-centered or single-gender options.[53]

With characteristic candor, she advises women leading in male-dominated spaces to learn to "navigate Guy World," noting that there is "an element of unspoken competitiveness," like a poker game, among powerful men. Women don't need to adopt this competitive style, but they do need to "read the room" to be effective.[54]

McGuire also counsels educational leaders not to let the elite set the agenda. Much of the public's focus on higher education, she notes ruefully, is still driven by Division I men's sports and *U.S. News* rankings.[55] Yet some of the most creative and powerful work happens in places ignored and demeaned by the press. "Remember always," McGuire told an audience of fellow minority-serving institutional leaders, that "the only thing that really matters is student growth and transformation." You have to be willing to just say no to *U.S. News*, stop apologizing, and tell your own story.

By telling her story, McGuire inspires others to embrace their calling as educators and lead with courage and conviction. Her long and impactful leadership journey is above all a love story. As she puts it in one of her favorite maxims, "Do what you love, love what you do, and work hard."[56]

Notes

1 Pat McGuire, in discussion with the author, May 25, 2018. All statements and direct quotes are taken from this interview unless otherwise noted. See also "24 Institutions Commit to Diversity and Inclusion through 2017 HHMI Inclusive Excellence Initiative," Howard Hughes Medical Institute, June 7, 2017, https://www.hhmi.org/news/24-institutions-commit-diversity-and-inclusion -through-2017-hhmi-inclusive-excellence.

2 "Theodore M. Hesburgh Award for Leadership Excellence: Honoring Patricia A. McGuire, President, Trinity Washington University," TIAA Institute, February 24, 2016, https://www.tiaa.org/public/pdf/2016_hesburgh_award _brochure.pdf; Celeste Ford, "2015 Academic Leadership Awards Announced," Carnegie Corporation of New York, September 24, 2015, https://www.carnegie .org/news/articles/carnegie-corporation-new-york-honors-four-higher -education-visionaries-winners-2015-academic-leadership-award/; Tony Pals, "Trinity Washington University President Patricia McGuire Receives Henry Paley Award for Service to Independent Higher Education," National Association of Independent Colleges and Universities press release, February 3, 2012, https://www.naicu.edu/news-events/news-from-naicu/2012/trinity -washington-university-president-patricia-m.

3 "President McGuire Honored by Association of Catholic Colleges and Universities," Trinity Washington University, February 5, 2018, https://www.trinitydc .edu/media/2018/02/05/president-mcguire-honored-association-of-catholic -colleges-universities/; "Honoring Patricia McGuire," Ignatian Solidarity Network, May 10, 2017, https://ignatiansolidarity.net/holstein/mcguire_2017/.

4 "Leader of the Years: A Tribute to President McGuire by Donald Graham," Trinity Washington University, May 15, 2007, https://www.trinitydc.edu/magazine -2007/leader-of-the-years-award/; Leslie Milk, "The Most Powerful Women in Washington," *Washingtonian*, October 2, 2017, https://www.washingtonian .com/2017/10/02/the-most-powerful-women-in-washington/.

5 "Academic Freedom Award," AAUP Updates, June 16, 2010, https://www.aaup .org/news/academic-freedom-award#.XDt47_Z2vD4.

6 Daniel de Vise, "The Devoted: She Spent Her Life Transforming Trinity. So Where Does Pat McGuire—and the University She Rebuilt—Go from Here?," *Washington Post*, February 14, 2010, W26, http://www.washingtonpost.com/ wp-dyn/content/article/2010/02/09/AR2010020902208.html??noredirect=on.

7 Kevin Carey, "The Sisters of Trinity: Many of America's Most Powerful Women Went to a College You've Never Heard Of," *Washington Monthly*, July–August 2011, https://washingtonmonthly.com/magazine/julyaug-2011/the-trinity -sisters/.

8 Ibid.

9 Ibid.

10 Ibid.

11 Ibid.

12 Ibid.

13 Ibid.
14 Pat McGuire, "Sustaining Soul While Shifting Paradigm: Trinity's Journey through Transformation," remarks, USA Funds Symposium, February 21, 2013, https://www.trinitydc.edu/president/files/2013/02/Sustaining-Institutional -Transformation-final-with-embedded-slides-for-posting-2-26-2013.pdf.
15 "Education: Sisterly Advice," *Time*, November 2, 1959, http://content.time .com/time/magazine/article/0,9171,892840,00.html.
16 Carey, "Sisters of Trinity."
17 De Vise, "Devoted."
18 Carey, "Sisters of Trinity."
19 Sister Margaret Claydon, speech, National Catholic Education Association, 1965. Cited by Pat McGuire, Twitter, May 27, 2016, https://twitter.com/ trinityprez/status/736249759346884609.
20 Carey, "Sisters of Trinity."
21 De Vise, "Devoted."
22 Pat McGuire, "Former Women's College Goes Co-ed, Fights to Stay Relevant," interview by Michel Martin, *Tell Me More*, NPR, February 15, 2010, https://www.npr.org/templates/story/story.php?storyId=123668459&t= 1539519726924.
23 De Vise, "Devoted."
24 Ibid.
25 Ibid.
26 Carey, "Sisters of Trinity."
27 McGuire, "Former Women's College."
28 De Vise, "Devoted."
29 McGuire, "Former Women's College."
30 Cited in de Vise, "Devoted."
31 Amy Argetsinger, "Reinventing Trinity," *Washington Post*, April 7, 2002, https://www.washingtonpost.com/archive/lifestyle/magazine/2002/04/07/ reinventing-trinity/6543a81a-a288-44cb-a323-ac84fe9105da/?noredirect=on& utm_term=.553c855f751a.
32 Pat McGuire, "How Can Mizzou Heal? A 1996 Incident Offers Some Lessons about Race," Hechinger Report, November 12, 2015, https://hechingerreport .org/how-can-mizzou-heal-a-1996-campus-incident-offers-some-lessons-about -race/.
33 Ibid.
34 Ibid.
35 Ibid.
36 Ibid.
37 McGuire, "Sustaining Soul," 8.
38 Quoted in ibid., 10.
39 Ibid., 9.
40 Ibid., 11.
41 Ibid., 5.
42 Argestinger, "Reinventing Trinity."

43 "Trinity at THEARC | About THEARC," Trinity Washington University, 2019, https://www.trinitydc.edu/thearc/about-thearc/.

44 De Vise, "Devoted."

45 Nick Anderson, "How This Women's College Got Its First New Academic Building in 50 Years," *Washington Post*, June 3, 2016, https://www.washingtonpost.com/news/grade-point/wp/2016/06/03/how-this-womens-college-got-its-first-new-academic-building-in-50-years/?utm_term=.03f37945f8ed.

46 Pat McGuire, "Teacher Regulations Worthy of George Orwell," *Huffington Post*, February 1, 2015, https://www.huffingtonpost.com/patricia-mcguire/teacher-regulations-worth_b_6590286.html?guccounter=1.

47 De Vise, "Devoted."

48 Gabe Bullard, "Area Catholic Leader Says Wuerl's Resignation Would Be a Step toward Healing," WAMU 88.5, August 21, 2018, https://wamu.org/story/18/08/21/area-catholic-leader-says-wuerls-resignation-step-toward-healing/.

49 Scott Jaschik, "Speaking Out When Others Wouldn't," *Inside Higher Ed*, February 20, 2017, https://www.insidehighered.com/news/2017/02/20/president-trinity-washington-outspoken-criticism-trump-administration-including.

50 Ibid.

51 "2010 Alexander Meiklejohn Award for Academic Freedom," AAUP Bulletin, 134–137, https://www.aaup.org/NR/rdonlyres/5E4DA45C-8C0A-40FB-AEF6-8D85C4614795/0/MeiklejohnAward.pdf.

52 Ibid.

53 Pat McGuire, "Imagining a World Unseen: Women's Colleges 2050," presentation, Wesleyan College Faculty Senate, March 26, 2010, https://www.trinitydc.edu/president/files/2010/10/WESLEYAN.pdf.

54 Ibid.

55 Ibid.

56 Brian Lamb, "Q&A with Patricia McGuire," C-SPAN, March 3, 2010, https://www.c-span.org/video/?292359-1/qa-pat-mcguire.

In Pursuit of Educational Access

Juliet García Leading from within the Bureaucracy, against the Grain

Maureen A. Mahoney

> I want us to be known, not because we are on the
> border and the sea, but because of what we believe
> to be important. That we exist in a community
> whose only option for significant gain is through
> education. I promise to give it all I've got. I require
> no less of the faculty, of the administrative officers,
> of the staff, of the student, and of the community.
> We are truly on our way, and I invite you to join us.
>
> —Juliet Villarreal García, inaugural address on
> becoming president of Texas Southmost College,
> April 1986

Juliet Villarreal García's life embodies her relentless commitment to opportunity and education without racial, economic, or geographic barriers. She grew up in a large extended family in Brownsville, Texas, surrounded by a strong community that enjoyed few economic or educational resources. When she was appointed president of Texas Southmost College (TSC), a community college, she became the first Mexican American woman in the United States to hold such a position.

Concerned about her students' lack of access to a four-year institution, she pioneered a plan to establish a campus for the University of Texas at Brownsville (UTB) based on a partnership with TSC. She was appointed founding president of the UTB/TSC partnership in January 1991. Without leaving home, she became an internationally recognized educator, affording access for tens of thousands of predominantly Hispanic students in the Rio Grande Valley—students who would otherwise not have dreamed of, let alone enjoyed, the opportunity to attend a four-year university. For two decades, she oversaw the partnership between UTB and TSC, worked with two boards (UT regents and TSC trustees), and navigated local, state, and national challenges, all the while insisting on a vision of her university as a site for "convening languages and cultures across boundaries."[1] Described by others as a "bold, visionary, determined, and passionate leader," she was named by *Time* magazine in 2010 as one of the top ten university presidents in the United States and by *Fortune* magazine in 2014 as one of the world's fifty greatest leaders.[2]

García's career was built around her conviction that she was best suited for effecting change by working within institutions. She comfortably incorporated the contradictions of her upbringing—that she should be a lady and also brainy, independent, and self-sufficient—into a leadership style that sought consensus and required compromise. But she never compromised her vision as she built a revolutionary hybrid institution to serve the goal of educational access for members of her community. Her extraordinary ability to navigate the demands of multiple constituencies in the service of her mission was continually tested. It was eventually brought to the brink of failure in 2008 by a crisis that foreshadowed heated debates about illegal immigration. Her response to the crisis was honed by her upbringing, education, and development as a leader in a range of work experiences that were both supportive and challenging.

Background

Dr. García's commitment to South Texas is in her bones. She was born and raised in Brownsville, the daughter of an American-born mother and a Mexican-born father. She describes both of her parents as "perfectly bilingual and biliterate," a phrase that describes her own accomplishment and her goal for her students. Neither of her parents had the opportunity to attend college, but they held fast to that ambition for their three children. Juliet was the middle child and the only daughter. The children enjoyed deep connections with multiple aunts and uncles in the area. Juliet notes, "[I was] blessed to have very accomplished women in my family," some of whom did graduate from college.[3]

Dr. García's mother died of breast cancer when she was nine years old. The women in her extended family provided support and schooling in what it meant to be a lady. At the same time, her father insisted on the children's independence and self-sufficiency. Shortly after his wife's death, he spoke to his children: "You have survived the hardest thing you will ever confront in your lives. . . . You are strong; you are survivors." His message to his only daughter was to be the "kind of woman my mother had been—smart and accomplished."[4] These narratives of strength and female competence remained compass points for Dr. García throughout her life.

Juliet García was sixteen when she graduated from high school. Concerned about her going away to college, her father insisted that she attend TSC, the local community college where she would later become president. She spent her sophomore year away from home at Southwest Texas State in San Marcos, Texas (now Texas State University). During that year, she became engaged to Oscar, a friend of her older brother. They were married a year later and moved to Houston so that Juliet could attend the University of Houston. Six months after graduation, she gave birth to her first child.

García did not consider herself a leader in college; when asked if she was, she responded, "Absolutely not." Her single extracurricular activity in college was the debate team at Southwest Texas State. Her debate partner was male, so she competed with the men's team, honing her rhetorical skills in a masculine environment. Looking back, she said, "It was probably the best possible training I could have gotten for what I was eventually to do in my career."[5]

After she earned her baccalaureate, García's husband suggested she study for a master's degree. She chose classical rhetoric and public address, skills that would prove a great advantage later in her career. Her second baby came several months after she started the master's program: "I became known as the pregnant Mexican among my cohort of graduate students at the University of Houston. . . . I remember thinking that I could prove to my professors that I was really very smart if I could just have a few days of sleep."[6]

García earned her undergraduate degree in January 1970 and her master's degree in May 1972. She was not politically engaged during these years of intense student activism, something about which she expresses a bit of embarrassment: "I suppose it was just that I was having babies and trying to finish my degrees. Life was turbulent enough."[7]

After completing her master's degree, García took a job teaching speech and diction at Pan American University in Edinburg, Texas, about an hour from Brownsville. To be certified for graduation, students were required to demonstrate that they had eliminated Spanish accents from their speech. Part of García's responsibility was to administer the speech test. She hated every minute of that work and, on one occasion, refused to certify a white student who spoke with a heavy drawl. After one semester, she was offered a job at TSC, where she had spent her first year in college. She was warned that she was committing professional suicide by moving from a university to a community college. But she could not continue to participate in a work environment that, in her words, "required me to be an accomplice to stripping people of their cultural identity."[8]

García's first job at TSC was in the English department. She was twenty-three years old. For a time, she concentrated on her new job and her young family. Soon, however, she became increasingly aware of TSC's paucity of resources. She wanted to position herself to be able to make a difference. She learned of a Ford Foundation fellowship for minority doctoral candidates and applied. She won the fellowship and enrolled at UT Austin in 1974. Her children were still preschoolers, and she made a commitment that the family would be back in Brownsville in time for the oldest to start first grade there. This gave her about two and a half years to earn the doctorate. By this time, she was clear on her goal to return to the Rio Grande Valley to improve education.

García's graduate mentor and dissertation advisor, Dr. Martin Todero, recognized her commitment and respected her goal. He helped her set a schedule that would enable her to earn her PhD within that short time frame. She was awarded the doctorate in communication and linguistics in 1976, after which she returned to TSC to teach.

García finally felt in a position to pursue advocacy in support of educational access. This commitment became the linchpin of her career. Her activism, though yet to be fully expressed, had been nurtured throughout her childhood by family stories of "using your voice and having the courage of your convictions."[9] When her grandfather, who lived with his family in Harlingen, Texas, got fed up with the city's segregated schools, he went to the school district office with his children and a shotgun, demanding that they be allowed to attend the Anglo school. According to the story, Juliet's mother and siblings were immediately enrolled.

García became a public activist after she returned to Brownsville for the second time. Her work began with her involvement in Valley Interfaith, a coalition of Catholic and Protestant congregations advocating for the rights of the poor. She gained recognition as an accomplished speaker and was selected to address Ross Perot and then governor Mark White on behalf of the organization. Her public activism set up a conflict and a turning point. The president of TSC was uncomfortable with her public persona, and García was called to his office. She expected to be fired, but instead, she was offered the deanship. This began her lifetime strategy of "working within the bureaucracy against the grain."[10] Her goals, however, never changed. She became a dean at TSC in 1981. Five years later, she was appointed president—the first female Mexican American to hold such a position in the United States.[11]

García's constituency in Brownsville was at least 90 percent Hispanic. As dean and then president, an important aspect of her job was to recruit students, and she was highly successful in increasing enrollment. Aware, however, that only 17 percent of community college students nationwide transferred to a four-year institution to gain a baccalaureate degree, she "worried about leading students down a path that would not be a good return on their and our [TSC's] investment." At the same time, she also knew that community colleges were the most common entry point for higher education for Latino students.

García became convinced that the only strategy for enhancing opportunity for the young people in her community was to establish a local four-year institution where her students could have access to advance their studies. Although there was a neighboring baccalaureate institution, Pan American University in Edinburg, its enrollment hovered over the years at one thousand students, and it did not provide the welcoming environment that Dr. García sought. Meanwhile, enrollment at TSC was increasing by double digits every year. García determined that her students would be well served by a streamlined transition to a university. She also was acutely aware that whatever plan she developed, the cost would have to be very low. Due to the falling price of oil in the 1980s, Texas was experiencing a marked drop in revenue. Furthermore, the Mexican peso had dropped in value by about 50 percent, and few people from either side of the border were spending, another factor in low tax revenues.

Dr. García and a supportive TSC board agreed to advocate for a "university on top of a community college." They set their sights on a University of Texas campus. The chair of the board, Mary Rose Cardenas, had the political connections to arrange a meeting with Hans Mark, then the chancellor of the UT system. Although Mark expressed support for the idea, he suggested a timeline of about fifteen to twenty years. Board Chair Cardenas responded that they would have to approach Texas A&M, the traditional rival of UT. García speculates that Chancellor Mark's competitive spirit led him to agree to read a proposal right away.

The idea was simple but radical. The university would be located on the site of TSC, the locally funded community college, so that the two campuses would become one. Revenue streams from TSC and UT would be combined. Buildings would be used in common, and staff, faculty, and library facilities would be shared, as would administrative costs such as insurance and maintenance of facilities and grounds. There would be a single president overseeing both institutions and reporting to the UT Board of Regents (appointed by the governor) as well as the TSC Board of Trustees (elected for six-year terms in local elections). This groundbreaking partnership would achieve García's lifetime mission of access to higher education for her region: community college students would benefit from an open admission policy providing access to a prestigious university that was located at home. All transfer barriers would be eliminated with open enrollment, and students would not be required to commute 250 miles to further their educations.

Obstacles had to be overcome before a final plan could be reached. For one thing, there seemed to be no legal foundation for a partnership between the university and a local entity. Fortuitously, attorney John Stafford, who was working on the project, unearthed a Texas law that had been passed in anticipation of another such partnership elsewhere in the state that had never been realized. That law established a precedent for the layered institution that the UT chancellor and the TSC board envisioned.

The plan was laid out and seemed within reach. With the leadership of the chair of the TSC board, Mary Rose Cardenas, along with another strong trustee proponent, Jean Eckhoff, the community college board was enthusiastic. They formed a powerful alliance with García to promote the ideals at the heart of the merger. All trustees were acutely aware that a partnership with UT would bring not only resources but prestige to the area.

State leadership and the board of regents were also ready to move forward. In García's words, "The authorizing environment was favorable." García and her TSC board were well networked. Chair Cardenas had been active in the Brownsville community for decades and had tremendous local knowledge and support. One member of the UT regents, Gene Powell, was from the Rio Grande Valley. The president of UT Laredo, also on the border, was a member as well. In addition, García had cultivated a relationship with then governor Ann Richards (they both owned vacation homes on South Padre Island).

Adding an important legal component, a class-action lawsuit had been filed against the state of Texas in 1987 by the League of United Latin American Citizens (*LULAC v. Richards*). The suit charged that Texas discriminated against its citizens in South Texas by not affording educational opportunities to them that were available to students in other regions of the state. The complainants eventually lost the case in the state supreme court. However, the suit is widely considered to be the impetus for the South Texas Border Initiative (STBI, 1989), legislation that pumped $880 million into nine border institutions between 1990 and 2003. The proposed UT at Brownsville would not only benefit from these funds but address the inequities identified in the lawsuit.[12]

The timing was ideal. There was strong support for the new hybrid university at the state and local levels. But governors, legislatures, UT chancellors, and boards are subject to change with every election. In García's words, "We needed to maintain authority in a very fragile moment." Negotiations were nearly complete when one major obstacle threatened the deal. TSC board chair Mary Rose Cardenas, in spite of her board's eagerness to finalize the agreement, insisted that she also have a "guarantee of leadership." In other words, she wanted final approval on the selection of the first president of the new UT at Brownsville/TSC. Without that guarantee, she believed she would be "giving away too much, and it would violate her oath as chair of the board of TSC." Her candidate for the presidency was the leader she had come to know and trust at TSC: Juliet García.

The university, by contrast, proposed that Homer Pena, then president of Pan American University, be appointed the president of the new university. Unbeknownst to Mary Rose Cardenas, Juliet García had already been offered the position of executive vice president of UT Brownsville, working under the UT chancellor's choice for president. This offer created a profound dilemma for her. The proposed president had been the leader of the local Pan American University for years without increasing its small enrollment or exercising his leadership to increase access to local Hispanic students. In addition, the privately communicated offer effectively isolated her from her biggest proponent, TSC chair Cardenas. On the other hand, the appointment would ensure García a senior administrative position in the institution she had fought to establish. She was continually mindful that the entire deal was fragile.

García considered the offer of the executive vice presidency, fully aware that her answer could either ensure or derail the proposed project. She discussed the offer with her husband, and twenty-five years later, she recalls his response: "You won't like it. You won't be in charge." Without consulting Mary Rose Cardenas, she turned down the offer. Upon hearing of García's decision, as García remembers the occasion, Cardenas responded, "You'd better turn it down! I'm glad you did." That issue was resolved, but the presidency of UT Brownsville was still in play.

Negotiations continued after García turned down the executive vice-chancellorship. Tensions ran high. The vice-chancellor from the university system, who was representing UT in the negotiations, was unwilling to have a local community college board chair dictate to UT what to do. He held to the position that the longtime president of Pan Am University be appointed the leader of the new UT Brownsville. Chair Cardenas maintained that the college was not going to trust its assets to just anyone. She insisted, García related to me, that the young, energetic Latina who had successfully led TSC be appointed. The impasse persisted to the point that the UT vice-chancellor walked out of a meeting.

He returned with a new idea. The president of Pan American University would be appointed the first president of the UT Brownsville, taking office in September 2000. He would hold the office for one semester. After that, García would assume the presidency. As García recalled the occasion, Cardenas and the TSC Board of Trustees agreed to the compromise. Nothing was put into writing, but the UT gave his word to work it out as Cardenas requested. Although then UT chancellor Hans Mark was annoyed by the insistence of the TSC board about the presidency, he often remarked later that he considered the work he did in Brownsville among the most important of his career.

In accordance with the verbal agreement, Homer Pena stepped down after one semester. García became president of the new UT Brownsville in January 2001. Among the myriad challenges, she needed to solve the problem of overall governance. After the merger, the UT Board of Regents would oversee the UT component, but the TSC board would continue to represent the interests of the local community on the TSC side. The unwieldiness of this structure was exacerbated by the need for the new university to be accredited by the Southern Association of Colleges and Schools. SACS accreditation required one governing board, not two. In García's words, "We needed the TSC board to participate as an advisory board but donate as a real board."

As García related to me, she navigated this problem by continuing to meet with the TSC board monthly as she had done before the merger. She also met with the board of regents quarterly, routine for all the presidents in the system. The UT regents held fast to the condition of having final say on the selection of all future presidential appointments. In the spirit of the merger, the TSC board agreed that although they would interview all the candidates, the final approval would be the university's. Commenting on this dual reporting arrangement, García said, "Working with both a locally elected board and the UT Board of Regents was always a delicate dance. . . . I lived a double life for those twenty years. . . . We often referred to ourselves as chameleons, able to shift from the community college world to the university world with ease when necessary."

Former UT chancellor Mark Yudof noted that "Juliet García [was] the linchpin—the glue that held it together—and was able to move easily between the usually disparate worlds of a community college and a university. She has credibility as a Latina and a PhD."[13]

García succeeded in managing this vulnerable coalition by developing three skills: unswerving focus on her mission, inspirational leadership, and courage to speak out. From the beginning, she was steadfast in her goal of affording educational access to students in the Rio Grande Valley. She mobilized her considerable narrative skills to motivate others to join her in the project: "I leaned in toward the better nature of ourselves and of board members. I inspired them with our work. We are teachers. We taught them our mission and purpose."

In spite of her upbringing, García's skills at forceful advocacy did not come easily. She credits three women role models on the TSC board with lending her courage early on. Jean Eckhoff, Mary Rose Cardenas, and Rosemary Breedlove were women on the board who themselves were outspoken in support of García's mission. "I often say," says García, "I borrowed their courage until I grew my own."

García maintained the strong support of the community college board even as she worked with the UT regents to develop her new campus. García and her TSC board led a successful bond initiative that increased revenue by doubling the local tax rate. This, along with funding from state Higher Education Assistance Funds (HEAF), allowed her to improve facilities and resources on the UT Brownsville / TSC campus. At the same time, she expanded faculty, staff, and library resources, all of which were fully shared by the university and community college. Most important, students moved seamlessly between the two institutions. Any community college student could enroll in the university without the barrier of additional application requirements and the review of credits already earned. Tens of thousands of students took advantage of this opportunity, and enrollment at the merged institution reached seventeen thousand. By the end of her tenure, UT Brownsville offered bachelor degrees in sixty-eight majors and hosted thirty-five master's programs and two PhD programs. Over the years, students became largely unaware of the distinction between the community college and the university.

The work of building the institution continued for sixteen years with President García negotiating compromises and agreements between the local community, the TSC board, and the university system. A threat came in October 2007 from an unexpected source: the Department of Homeland Security (DHS) under President George W. Bush. Bush signed into law the Secure Fence Act of 2006, authorizing the construction of hundreds of miles of barriers on the Mexican border for the purpose of controlling illegal immigration.[14] García received a letter from the DHS seeking permission to build an eighteen-foot barricade through the middle of her campus. The proposed path of the wall would render a large part of the campus unavailable, including the golf course and international technology center.[15] García believed that it would threaten the security of her campus and complicate access for her students.

Even more important to García than the loss of resources and threat to security was the symbolism that a wall would create. Such a visible obstruction would interrupt García's vision of an open, international educational space and access at the center of her mission. Hardly believing that the DHS demand was serious, her first impulse was to ignore the letter and keep it to herself.

Several weeks later, the DHS sent a follow-up letter threatening to sue both García and UT system chancellor Mark Yudof. The entire university system was now implicated. Even in her uncertainty about whether she could expect support from the central office, her opposition to the wall never faltered. As a result, she became embroiled in a highly public legal controversy that drew in both the TSC Board of Trustees and the UT regents. The UT legal team was called in. García was confident that her local board of trustees would understand what was at stake, and indeed, they were highly supportive of her. However, she needed the backing of Chancellor Yudof and the UT regents as well. García recalls, "If I had had a TSC board that wanted one thing and regents that wanted something else, we would have been in a terrible quandary. The local board was as outraged as I was, so I had to convince the regents, the chancellor, and the general counsel. I tested the very edges of this complicated governing structure. If the chancellor had said, 'You are on your own,' it would have raised the question of whether the partnership and my presidency could . . . survive."

It was a great relief, García said, when Mark Yudof, former dean of the law school at UT Austin and a constitutional expert, expressed full support of García's position.

García refused to allow DHS surveyors on the UT Brownsville campus. In response, DHS sued UT Brownsville, and the University of Texas initiated a series of legal maneuvers that dragged on for months. The DHS suit was settled in federal court in March 2008 with an agreement that the DHS would be allowed to survey the campus on the condition that it would engage in discussions with

UT Brownsville to consider alternatives to the wall. The DHS did not live up to the bargain. In June, Border Patrol chief Ron Vitiello called the court-mandated discussion of alternatives a waste of time. DHS spokesperson Laura Keehner stated that the department could not wait around forever.[16]

The DHS notified UT on June 6 that they would begin construction of the wall without consultation. In response, UT and TSC filed a motion demanding compliance with the terms of the March 2008 agreement. Subsequently, a judge ordered the DHS to work with UT to find a solution. Public debate continued as well. Outspoken criticism of the wall came from environmental groups, Native groups, human rights groups, and border cities.[17] The mayor of Brownsville expressed strong opposition. President García became a reluctant public voice in resistance to the wall. According to *Diverse Issues in Higher Education*, "The university and its two-year sister school TSC [were] the most formidable opponent of a border fence that [was] widely unpopular in the Rio Grande Valley."[18] García testified at a congressional hearing in 2008 that "she had not been consulted" about the fence and that it would pose "serious harm to the university on many fronts, including risks to public safety, to its property investments and to its educational mission."[19]

The wall had vehement supporters as well as opponents, García told me. As she found herself at the center of the controversy, she understood that she might be the object of ad hominem attacks from the DHS and others. She worried that her family was vulnerable as well. She and her husband spoke to their adult children explaining that the DHS would build a dossier on all of them. The parents were confident that there were no secrets in their own histories that the DHS could turn against them. They needed to know if any issues might arise due to the children's past behavior. Their children assured them there was nothing.

One day in July 2008, García said, she received a phone call from Mark Yudof and UT's general counsel informing her that she had one week to settle the matter. Yudof feared he could no longer count on the support of members of the board of regents, all of whom were by that time Republican appointees of then governor Rick Perry.

García scheduled a meeting with the DHS in Washington, DC, in the hope of negotiating a settlement. She still did not have a resolution in mind.

Resolution

Shortly before leaving for Washington, García gathered her team on the levee on campus where the DHS wanted to build the wall. As they gazed out on the landscape, one member of the group observed that they already had a wall in the form of a fence that had been built a century earlier. They developed a proposal to reinforce the existing fence but retain ownership of the property and have final say over what the structure would look like. Armed with this compromise proposal, García and the UT general counsel went to Washington.

They were led to a conference room deep in the DHS building. García recalls the armed guards and the photographs on the walls of people being detained. She was the only woman at the meeting. Her sense was that the DHS staff were tired of the issue. García presented her proposal. Although she was offering to build a "wall," her goal was to preserve the welcoming nature of the campus. The way to do that would be to bolster the fence and integrate it into the campus architecture. She envisioned a ten-foot fence rather than an eighteen-foot one. She imagined vines covering the structure. She insisted that there be no gate where papers could be checked. The DHS insisted that it be ram-proof and that security cameras be installed. An agreement was reached.

Still, there was one more hurdle. The federal court in Brownsville needed to approve the plan. García understood that her faculty was worried about the outcome of the decision. She requested a meeting with the U.S. Senate, she recalled, and explained that although the university might win or lose, it was still important to teach students advocacy in the public arena.

García went to court in late July 2008, backed by UT attorneys. When she arrived, she was surprised to see approximately ten local attorneys in the audience, providing support for her with their presence. On July 31, 2008, Federal Judge Hanen approved the agreement. The crisis was resolved.[20] Subsequently, García reflected on her experience:

> The University of Texas at Brownsville and TSC shares the commitment of the U.S. Congressional and executive branches to protect our country. We know that America's security is a national responsibility. However, we also know that what is needed is authentic security, which can only be achieved by deploying all of our assets, including fully resourced enforcement, a stable economy, trustworthy and open governance, and an educated citizenry. . . . My life's work has been spent trying to guarantee that the next generation has access to an education and becomes vested in protecting, participating in, and defending this democracy. It has been my duty to be a good steward not only of the resources entrusted to me but also of the values and principles of our democracy.[21]

Nine years later, the "wall" is an unobtrusive feature of the campus, covered with flowering vines.

At times, the controversy over the wall tested García's confidence that she could keep the partnership between TSC and UT together and also hold to her lifelong mission of a boundary-free educational zone. She prevailed with her usual persistence, negotiation skills, and faith in her principles. Several years later, however, another challenge arose that would prove insurmountable. Mary Rose Cardenas, García's longtime supporter on the TSC board, had stepped down. Subsequent local elections resulted in profound turnover on the board, including individuals who "ran to disrupt instead of to build." Eventually, the disruptors held the majority vote. As the original partnership agreement was being reviewed, they questioned its terms and efficacy.

At first, García was confident that she could mobilize her teaching skill and facility at narrative persuasion to inspire the new board members. Multiple teaching efforts, including twelve workshops in which García presented the evidence, for the first time proved ineffective. The new board majority was fixated on their loss of authority in the original partnership agreement; they did not support the cornerstone concept of one governing board as a condition of accreditation. UT Chancellor Francisco Cigarroa stepped in to advocate for the partnership he knew was operating successfully and benefiting the citizens of the Rio Grande Valley. He, too, was unable to persuade the dissenting board members. In 2010, the TSC Board of Trustees voted to dissolve the partnership.[22] "In the end," García says, "it all came down to a desire to regain total local power and authority."

As the president of UT Brownsville, now unaffiliated with TSC, García was left with the heartbreaking task of dismantling the partnership that she had devoted her life to building. Everything had to be disentangled: the land, the buildings, the staff, the faculty, the students, and the open enrollment agreement. Hundreds of employees were laid off. García carried out her responsibility. She says, "I had many conversations with God. I said, 'They can have it, but why do I have to rip it apart?' It is the most difficult thing I have ever done."

García also participated in conversations about the future of her university. UT agreed to establish a new institution, the University of Texas Rio Grande Valley (UTRGV). The new institution would be eligible for significantly more state funding and would include the first medical school in the region. It would not, however, have an open-door agreement with a community college. Understanding the many benefits of UTRGV, García nevertheless believed that it needed new leadership. She declined to seek the presidency.

Notes

1 Juliet García, in discussion with the author, March 7, 2017. All direct quotes and statements are taken from this interview unless otherwise noted.

2 "Profile of Dr Juliet V Garcia, UTB President," YouTube video uploaded by UTBrownsville, June 19, 2015, https://www.youtube.com/watch?v=AtOZW _BjKnU; "The 10 Best College Presidents," *Time*, 2010, http://content.time .com/time/specials/packages/completelist/0,29569,1937938,00.html; "The World's 50 Greatest Leaders," *Fortune*, March 20, 2014, http://fortune.com/ 2014/03/20/worlds-50-greatest-leaders/.

3 Juliet García, in discussion with the author, January 11, 2017.

4 Ibid.

5 Ibid.

6 Ibid.

7 Ibid.

8 Ibid.

9 Ibid.

10 Ibid.

11 Regina D. Biddings-Muro, "The Courage to Lead: The Journey of the First Mexican American Woman College President in the U.S." (PhD diss., Benedictine University, April 2015).

12 Ricardo Ray Oregon, "LULAC vs. Richards: The Class Action Law Suit That Prompted the South Texas Border Initiative and Enhanced Access to Higher Education for Mexican Americans Living along the South Texas Border" (PhD diss., Northeastern University, 2013); A. Kauffman, "Commentary: Lawsuit Leads to Improvements in Texas Border Higher Education," *Monitor* (McAllen, Tex.), May 29, 2016.

13 Quoted by Juliet García, in discussion with the author, March 14, 2017.

14 Secure Fence Act of 2006, H.R. 6061, 109th Cong (2006).

15 "University of Texas Sues DHS Over Border Fence," *Homeland Security Newswire*, June 24, 2008.

16 Ibid.

17 Denise Gilman, "Obstructing Human Rights: The Texas-Mexico Border Wall," Working Group on Human Rights and the Border Wall, June 2008, https://law .utexas.edu/humanrights/borderwall/analysis/briefing-INTRODUCTION.pdf.

18 "Homeland Security and UT Brownsville Reach Accord on Campus Border Fence," *Diverse Issues in Higher Education*, August 6, 2008, http:// diverseeducation.com/article/11515/.

19 R. C. Archibold and Julia Preston, "Homeland Security Stands by Its Fence," *New York Times*, May 21, 2008.

20 Lynn Brezofsky, "Deal Means Border Fence Won't Split UT-Brownsville Campus," *San Antonio Express*, July 31, 2008, https://www.chron.com/news/ houston-texas/article/Deal-means-border-fence-won-t-split-1756974.php.

21 Juliet García, "The Path to Settlement between University of Texas Brownsville and the U.S. Department of Homeland Security," letter to the Inter-American Commission of Human Rights, Organization of American States, October 22, 2008, https://repositories.lib.utexas.edu/handle/2152/15706.

22 Reeve Hamilton, "After 20 Years, a Messy Divorce in Brownsville," *Texas Tribune*, November 4, 2011, https://www.texastribune.org/2011/11/04/after-20 -years-messy-divorce-brownsville.

Acknowledgments

We have many to thank for bringing this book into reality. First, we are grateful to Rutgers University Press for their commitment to *Women Leaders in Higher Education* as a volume in the Junctures in Leadership series. Our sincere thanks to Kimberly Guinta, editorial director, and Mary Trigg, chair, women's and gender studies, for their guidance and support pulling this team together after the untimely loss of Dr. Alison R. Bernstein, whose vision continues to inspire this work. For her insightful and critical comments on early drafts, we thank Marjorie Feinson, PhD, and for her valuable queries and edits in preparing the manuscript, we thank Marti Hagan.

We thank all the contributing authors who brought their experience, intellect, and academic rigor to each chapter. All this would have been impossible without the enthusiastic participation of the women leaders profiled. Finally, we give a special note of thanks and gratitude to Jasper Chang, Rutgers University Press editorial assistant, for his invaluable expertise and stewardship throughout the entire production of this book.

Carmen Twillie Ambar
President, Oberlin College

Carol T. Christ
President, University of California, Berkeley

Michele Ozumba
President (former), Women's College Coalition

Contributors

CARMEN TWILLIE AMBAR is the fifteenth president of Oberlin College and the first African American leader in the institution's 185-year history. Ambar came to Oberlin in 2017 after serving nine years as president of Cedar Crest College in Allentown, Pennsylvania. Prior to Cedar Crest, Ambar served as vice president and dean of Douglass College at Rutgers University. Before Rutgers, she served as assistant dean of graduate education at the Woodrow Wilson School of Public and International Affairs at Princeton University. As an attorney, she worked in the New York City Law Department as an assistant corporation counsel. President Ambar is a native of Little Rock, Arkansas, and is the mother of twelve-year-old triplets, Gabrielle, Luke, and Daniel.

SUSAN C. BOURQUE is the Esther Booth Wiley 1934 Professor Emerita of Government at Smith College and a former director of the Smith Project on Women and Social Change. She served as Smith's provost and dean of the faculty from 2001 to 2009.

CAROL T. CHRIST began her term as the eleventh chancellor of the University of California, Berkeley, on July 1, 2017. A celebrated scholar of Victorian literature, Christ is also well known as an advocate for quality, accessible public higher education; a proponent of the value of a broad education in the liberal arts and sciences; and a champion of women's issues and diversity on college campuses. Christ spent more than three decades as a professor and administrator at UC Berkeley before serving as president of Smith College, one of the country's most distinguished liberal arts colleges, from 2002 to 2013. Prior to joining Smith, Christ served as UC Berkeley's executive vice-chancellor and provost from 1994 until 2000. Christ received her BA from Douglass College and her MPh and PhD from Yale University.

LESLEE A. FISHER is a professor and the director of the sport psychology and motor behavior graduate program at the University of Tennessee. She holds a PhD in sport psychology (UC Berkeley), an MEd in counselor education (University of Virginia), an MS in education (University of Michigan), and a BS in education (University of Michigan). Fisher is also a fellow in the Association for Applied Sport Psychology (AASP), served as AASP's secretary/treasurer, is a Certified Mental Performance Consultant (CMPC), a member of the American Psychological Association, and a registrant on the U.S. Olympic Committee's Sport Psychology Registry. In her spare time, she likes to hang out in her she shed in Key West, Florida, and write.

ELIZABETH KISS has served as the warden of Rhodes House at the University of Oxford and CEO of the Rhodes Trust since 2018. Prior, Kiss served for twelve years as the president of Agnes Scott College in Atlanta, Georgia. During her tenure, Agnes Scott College broke records for enrollment and retention and was named the second "Most Diversified College in America" by *Time* and the country's most successful liberal arts college for graduating low-income students by the U.S. Department of Education. In December 2017, the *Chronicle of Higher Education* named Elizabeth Kiss in its 2017 list of the most influential people in U.S. higher education. From 1997 to 2006, Kiss served as the founding director of Duke University's Kenan Institute for Ethics, building a university-wide interdisciplinary center focused on promoting moral reflection and commitment in personal, professional, organizational, and civic life. Her academic focus has been on moral and political philosophy, and she has published on moral education, human rights, ethnic conflict, nationalism, feminist theory, and transitional justice. Kiss received her BA in philosophy, magna cum laude, from Davidson College in North Carolina, where she became Davidson's first female Rhodes scholar, going on to receive a BPhil and DPhil from the University of Oxford.

KAREN R. LAWRENCE served as president of Sarah Lawrence College for a decade. In 2018, she was appointed as president of the Huntington Library, Art Collections, and Botanical Gardens, a collections-based research and educational institution serving scholars and the public in San Marino, California. From 1998 to 2007, Lawrence served as the dean of humanities at the University of California, Irvine. She has written widely on twentieth-century British and Irish literature, women experimental writers, and women and travel. Lawrence currently serves on the board of the National Humanities Center and is a member of the International Women's Forum.

JACQUELYN LITT is dean of Douglass Residential College and the Douglass Campus and is a professor of sociology as well as women's and gender studies at Rutgers University. Litt received her PhD in sociology from the University of Pennsylvania. Litt has been leading Douglass since 2010 and has been instrumental in ensuring Douglass's future as an intellectual community for undergraduate women at Rutgers. Her work to build new opportunities for students to share diverse perspectives was recognized in 2016 with the Leaders in Faculty Diversity Award at Rutgers University. She has been honored by the New Jersey State Senate and New Jersey State Assembly for her leadership and research at Douglass.

MAUREEN A. MAHONEY is dean of the college emerita and retired vice president for campus life at Smith College. Prior to that, she was a professor of psychology at Hampshire College. She holds a BA from the University of California, Santa Cruz, and a PhD in developmental psychology from Cornell University. Her scholarly interests center on development in context: the roles that social and historical location play in the emergence of subjectivity and the understanding of self and other. She has focused on personal narratives as they are shaped by and in turn shape cultural and family stories.

MICHELE OZUMBA is the former president of the Women's College Coalition (WCC), a nonprofit membership organization of women's colleges and universities in the United States and Canada. Her previous senior executive roles include president and CEO of Women's Funding Network (WFN), a philanthropic organization representing 160 women-led foundations across the globe, and president and CEO of the Georgia Campaign for Adolescent Power and Potential (GCAPP), a statewide nonprofit organization focused on adolescent reproductive health. Earlier in her career, Ozumba was a senior lecturer in urban planning and estate management at the University of Nigeria, teaching urban planning and land use economics, and was the first woman to serve as the department chair. In recognition of her nonprofit leadership, Ozumba was featured among *Fast Company*'s "League of Extraordinary Women 2012." Ozumba graduated from Douglass College with a bachelor's in history and political science and from Rutgers University with a master's in city and regional planning.

PATRICIA A. PELFREY is a senior research associate emerita at the Center for Studies in Higher Education at the University of California, Berkeley. She is the author of *Entrepreneurial President: Richard Atkinson and the University of California* (2012), coauthor of *A Brief History of the University of California* (with Margaret Cheney; 2004), and the editor of *The Pursuit of Knowledge: Speeches and Papers of Richard C. Atkinson* (2007). Her current research interests include women's leadership in higher education, the evolution of the American research university, and nineteenth-century ideas about knowledge, cognition, and education and their relation to contemporary thinking about universities.

MARILYN R. SCHUSTER earned her BA from Mills College and her MPhil and PhD in French language and literature from Yale University. She joined the faculty at Smith College in Northampton, Massachusetts, in 1971, and in 1981, she helped create the Smith College Program for the Study of Women and Gender. She was named the Andrew W. Mellon Professor in the Humanities and served as provost and dean of the faculty. She has written about curriculum transformation and contemporary women writers. She has been a professor and provost emerita since 2015 and resides in Oakland, California.

TYLER SLOAN is a student at the City University of New York (CUNY) School of Law, where she is pursuing a JD with a focus on gender- and criminal-justice issues in her hometown of New York City. She currently serves as board chair for CUNY Law's Lawyering for Reproductive Justice Group and advocates for survivors of domestic violence through the Sanctuary for Families' Courtroom Advocacy Project. During summer 2020, she is working as a judicial intern for U.S. magistrate judge Lois Bloom for the Eastern District of New York. Sloan graduated from Oberlin College in 2017 with high honors in politics for her thesis on the Supreme Court and abortion access. As an undergraduate, she was editor-in-chief of the school newspaper and a scholar-athlete for the women's varsity soccer team. She enjoys taking long bike rides, going to museums, and spending time with friends and family.

KAREN R. STUBAUS is the vice president of academic affairs at Rutgers University. A Phi Beta Kappa graduate of Douglass College, Stubaus holds a PhD in seventeenth-century American history. Over the course of her Rutgers career, she has been involved in a broad array of academic, budgetary, strategic, and policy matters across the university's three geographic locations in New Brunswick, Newark, and Camden as well as for Rutgers Biomedical and Health Sciences. Faculty affairs and academic labor relations have always been areas of particular interest to her. She has been instrumental in increasing the diversity of the faculty and in promoting women's leadership at all levels of the institution. She was centrally involved in the development and implementation of the first New Brunswick campus strategic plan in over two decades and in the full academic and policy integration of Rutgers University and the University of Medicine and Dentistry of New Jersey, the largest academic merger in the nation's history.

Index